God's Promises on wealth Series

How To Become
A
Millionaire
In A Way That Is
Dignifying To God

Volume One

Abimbola Cole Idris

T0128876

Testimonies from readers

"Abimbola Cole again delivers. She successfully solidifies her place among the greatest motivational writers with another breakthrough in the realm of motivational books. 'How to become a millionaire in a way that is dignifying to God' offers simple and effective principles that could be implemented into my day to day life. Also it alleviates my fear in knowing that what I am doing is done in a way that is pleasing and magnifies God."

Ahmed Idris from United Kingdom

Abimbola Cole Idris your book titled "How to conquer the spirit of fear and become a Millionaire" is a winner. It conveys a wealth of information and it is value for money.

Stephen from United Kingdom

Truly superb. Abimbola Cole Idris delivers the principles of being a millionaire in an innovative and provoking way that is bound to change anybody else's life also. I am truly grateful for having read this book. Abimbola Cole's Book is unquestionably up there with the likes of Rich Dad Poor Dad.

Daniel Billios from Greece

HOW TO BECOME A MILLIONAIRE IN A AWAY THAT IS DIGNIFYING TO GOD

Volume one

A motivational and spirit filled book that will help you become successful, prosperous and wealthy.

BY

ABIMBOLA   COLE   IDRIS

Same author of best selling book of all times called 'HOW TO SPRING FROM A NOBODY TO A MILLIONAIRE'

GOD's PROMISES PUBLICATION

iUniverse, Inc.
New York   Bloomington

HOW TO BECOME A MILLIONAIRE IN A WAY THAT IS DIGNIFYING TO GOD (VOLUME 1) REVISED AND UPGRADED COPY

iUniverse books may be ordered through booksellers or by contacting:

iUniverse
1663 Liberty Drive
Bloomington, IN 47403
www.iuniverse.com
1-800-Authors (1-800-288-4677)

Because of the dynamic nature of the Internet, any Web addresses or links contained in this book may have changed since publication and may no longer be valid. The views expressed in this work are solely those of the author and do not necessarily reflect the views of the publisher, and the publisher hereby disclaims any responsibility for them.

ISBN: 978-1-4401-3064-9 (pbk)
ISBN: 978-1-4401-3065-6 (ebk)

Printed in the United States of America

iUniverse rev. date: 4/2/2009

Reference: The following people has inspired me and I found their advices very useful.

Mark Victor Hansen, Robert Kiyosaki, Robert Allen, Mike Litman.

These people are great leaders and genius of our times.

DEDICATION

This book is dedicated to the Lord Jesus Christ who is my Lord and personal saviour, The Holy Spirit who is my Chairman and my silent director. He has entrusted this revelation into my hands.

My husband and our four children: Ahmed, Wole, Teslim and Rasheedah.

Also to all my readers and everybody that has helped in making this dream a reality.

I love you all and God bless.

CONTENTS

INTRODUCTION

What is prosperity?

Prosperity means to be successful, to be correct. It means to be right and to have money. Prosperity is to become a millionaire and to be aligned with certain requirements. These includes good health, having children, long life and many more blessing that comes from God.

What did God say about your prosperity?

The bible says in, Psalm 35:27 *"Let them shout for joy and be glad, who favour my righteous cause, and let them say continually, let the Lord be magnified, who has pleasure in the prosperity of His servant"*.

God has pleasure in your prosperity. Do not allow anybody or your present circumstance to deceive you? God wants you to prosper. He wants you to make money and become a millionaire, and to be a blessing to the gospel of Jesus Christ and also to all those people who are around you.

Once you have made your ways right in the sight of God, it is God's delight to prosper you. God will make you rich. There is no doubt about it. He will give you ideas that will turn you into a multi-millionaire so that you can bring glory to his name. Some become fearful when they are wealthy, thinking that they are robbing other people of their wealth.

Do not be afraid when you prosper

Do not be afraid for it is God's wish for you to prosper. God said in his unfailing word *"above all things I wish that you prosper as your soul prospers"* 3 John 2. Therefore if you are prospering you owe no apology to no one because you are only doing what your Father in Heaven commanded you to do.

Let us look into more scriptures that tell you about God's plan for your prosperity.

God is delighted in your prosperity.

If they obey and serve Him (GOD) they shall spend their days in prosperity, and their years in pleasures" - Job 36:11.

Prosperity is your birthright:

My friend, I am sure you understand what the above scripture is saying to you. It says that prosperity is your birthright. All you have to do in order to qualify is to obey and serve God.

In order for us to be crystal clear on the issue of the kind of prosperity God has in mind for you, let us analyse one more scripture on this topic.

In 1st Kings 10:7, the bible says *"However, I did not believe the words until I came and saw with my own eyes and indeed the half was not told me. Your wisdom and prosperity exceed the fame of which I heard"*. This is the type of prosperity that the Lord has for you. It is the type of prosperity that no one has ever heard about.

My brother and sister in Christ, God has a plan for your prosperity which was put in place from the beginning of creation.

Now that you have a deep understanding of what prosperity is, and what God says about your prosperity, we will continue on this adventure to see and hear the mind of God on what He has in stock for you in this book.

The Holy Spirit inspired me and gave me thirty-six principles you need to apply into your life in order for you to prosper and become a millionaire in a way that is pleasing to God.

God says in his word, *"My people are perishing because of lack of knowledge"* in other words my people are not making enough money as I God wished for them because they don't know how to go about it in the right way.

In response to God's command, and under the leadership of the Holy Spirit I have decided to give you these thirty-six principles that must be applied in order for you to prosper as a child of God. I will also give you seven scriptures that God has given me to support each principle He has given me for you. This will help to make it clearer to you that God truly wants you to prosper in a dignifying way.

I know that putting thirty-six principles in one book will be too big, I prayed and asked the Holy Spirit how to go about it. He then instructed me to divide it into volumes.

So I have started with this book, titled "*How To Become A Millionaire In A Way That Is Dignifying To God*". This will be volume one. We will have two to three more volumes to complete the thirty-six principles that God has shown me. I believe this will truly make you prosperous in the way God has ordained for you in Jesus name.

God has provided all these blessings for:

- Your enjoyment.
- Answers to any difficult situation you may be dealing with.
- What you can invest your money on in order to become a millionaire.
- What you need to do in order to qualify for a thousand fold breakthrough.

May the Lord quicken your understanding of His words In Jesus Name?

CHAPTER ONE

Principle #1: You must seek first the kingdom of God and every other thing shall be added unto you.

The first principle you need to apply in your life in order for you to prosper and become a millionaire is to, *"seek first the kingdom of God and every other thing shall be added unto you"*.

Remember, once we put God first every other thing shall be added unto us.

Scripture one in support of principle #1:

Matthew 6: 33 Jesus said *"seek first the kingdom of God and His righteousness and every other thing shall be added unto you"*.

The above scripture is your main key to becoming a millionaire.

In other words, Jesus is saying in this scripture that you should put God's kingdom first. He said make God's will and purposes your first priority and the following miracles shall follow you:

- Miracle of prosperity.
- Miracle of healing.
- Miracle of breakthrough.
- Miracle of joy and peace and many more.

Prosperity is your birthright, this is secret number one. Beloved, it is the first key to your becoming a millionaire. You must know and believe this in your heart.

My prayer for you:

My dear brother and sister, I pray in the mighty name of our Lord Jesus Christ that the Holy Spirit who lives big in you will begin to shine his light on the inside of you from this moment henceforth. I pray that you will always seek God's mind first in everything you endeavour to lay your hands on. For the bible says if you do all these you will prosper. God has prospered you in Jesus name. Amen.

Now pray this prayer aloud for yourself:

Lord Jesus, I believe in you, I adore you and I also believe that you are the Son of God. Lord send your Holy Spirit to come and start dwelling inside me. Help me to surrender all to God. Give me the strength to be able to seek first the kingdom of God before any of my undertakings, In Jesus name I have prayed. Amen.

Hint: - You need various streams of income flowing into your life, not just one or two.

Income means money received periodically, be it monthly or yearly, from one's work, land or investment.

Let us see what we can gain from the next scripture.

You need God to open your eyes. Therefore you must seek Him first in every thing you intend to do.

Scripture two in support of principle #1:

The bible says *"Open my eyes that I may see wondrous things from your laws"* - Psalm 119:18.

Make it your priority to seek God's face in prayers everyday. As you do this, God will open the eyes of your mind, so that you are able to know and understand what His will is concerning you in every situation and circumstance you encounter in life. He will also enlighten your path as to the right decisions you need to take for your way to be prosperous.

As you begin to put God first, by making it your priority to find out His will, as you read His words daily, He will begin to open your eyes. You will start seeing wondrous things from His word which will give you ideas and wisdom on how to prosper.

God will give you ideas on how to make wealth. He will also give you ideas on how to make money and become a millionaire in a godly way.

The next step is to know how to release God's hands upon your wealth.

How do you automatically release God's hand upon your money? It is easy. This is all you need to do:

- Start supporting the gospel.
- Win souls for Jesus Christ.
- Touch lives with your money, help the widow.
- Be generous to people, especially the poor and needy.
- Sponsor motherless children and orphanages and help build schools for them.
- Shelter the homeless.
- Give gifts to the hopeless and there are so many good causes you can support, all to the glory of God.

We all know that if you have no money you cannot help anyone. But as you desire in faith and start doing the little you can now to help others, God will see your heart and he will begin to bless you even more so that you can continue to be a blessing to others.

Prophetic words.

Beloved, God is about to release His abundant wealth upon you. You are about to experience the Lord's mighty hand.

He is about to release a thousand fold prosperity onto your life. Your breakthrough is knocking on your door. Prosperity is running after you. Ideas are coming your way. Money is making its way to you.

Now is your time, be ready to receive your wealth. There are parcels of wealth with your name written on them, all you need to do is to receive them. They are your entitlement, and yours to keep forever. Therefore, collect them right now and start enjoying them.

Now let us support the prophetic words with some prayers.

My Prayer for You:

By virtue of my role as a pastor and a prophetess of the Lord Jesus Christ, I declare that prosperity is your portion. I decree that you will no longer lack or beg for bread. I pray that you will be above only and never be beneath. I decree over you that the windows of heaven shall open for your sake. I pronounce that you will move to a higher level and your life will never be the same again in Jesus name, Amen.

Your Own Confession of Faith:

Please always open your mouth and speak out your prayer in faith. This is because the creative power of Gods word begins when you speak out in faith.

So now open your mouth and pray loud for yourself and your family.

1. Every Generational curse in my life from the lineage of my father or mother I command you to disappear in the mighty name of Jesus Christ.

2. I fire my spiritual arrow into every blockage in the way of my financial breakthrough in Jesus Name.

3. I release the fire of the Holy Ghost to burnout completely every stubborn spirit standing in the way of my prosperity.

4. I pray for God's wisdom on all I do and every step I take.

5. Thank you Lord for blessing the work of my hands in Jesus name.

Hint: - Your source of income needs to be a continuous stream not a one off. You need to make up your mind that it is alright for you to make and enjoy money in millions.

Let's study the next scripture together.

Scripture three in support of principle #1:

How to recognise the presence of God while you are seeking Him in your finances, and about what businesses you need to do?

1st Kings 19:11-13 God said to Elijah *"Go out and stand on the mountain before the Lord" and behold the Lord passes by and a great and strong wind tore into the mountains and broke the rocks into pieces before the Lord, but the Lord was not in the wind. And after the wind an earthquake, but the Lord was not in the earthquake. And after the earthquake a fire but the Lord was not in the fire, and after the fire a still small voice.*

*"A still small voice" this is where we are going, read it loud "**a still small voice**".*

So where is God then?

Beloved, as you begin to carefully listen to God through His words by reading the bible, every answer to the questions that you have always wanted to ask Him regarding your finances and prosperity will start coming to you.

You will begin to hear God in a ***still small voice*** saying to you: "my child what about that real estate business?

"How about becoming an industrialist?" "What about becoming a manufacturer of different products?" What about becoming a dimensionalist?" "How would you like to become someone who is writing plans for people's businesses and solving their business problems?

And as you do the above things, you will begin to make money because money is the reward for solving problems. The more problems you solve for people the more money you will make until you become a millionaire. The bible says about Jacob that "*the man grew exceedingly **prosperous** and came to own large flocks, and maidservants and menservants, and camels and donkeys-* Genesis 30:43.

He became prosperous and he used some of his money to give water to a thirsty Nation, because our God blessed him. God wants to do the same for you.

Let me pray with you:

Father Lord in heaven, I thank you. Holy Spirit I adore you. Father I give you honour. God I give you all adoration. Father I believe that you have chosen me to bring the good news of prosperity to your people. And you have also chosen me to tell your people how to become a millionaire in a way that is pleasing to you.

Therefore, by virtue of my role as a prophetess, I pray that your people will begin to experience your powerful hands in their lives the moment they lay their hands on this book. They will begin to prosper as never before and their lives shall never be the same again. Amen.

Now confess by faith and pray the following prayers for yourself.

God, I believe by faith that you have sent your words to bring me the good news of my breakthrough and how I can become a millionaire, which is the desire of my heart.

I am determined to follow the principles in this book as laid down in your word. Father, thank you, for you have blessed me and my family with your joy and goodness, in Jesus name, Amen

Hint: - Wealth is when small efforts produce big results. Poverty is when big efforts produce small results. You need to look around you, find out what problems the people are facing at the moment and begin to offer some solutions. Concentrate all your positive energy on problem solving and people will be willing to pay you for the solution which you have provided.

You need a product or service of your own in the market.

You also need to put a system in place, which will make your prospects hunger for your product or services. Now say this prayer out in faith: Lord God Almighty I thank you because you have created a hunger and thirst in the hearts of people for my goods and services in Jesus name. Amen.

Now let us learn from the next scripture.

Scripture four in support of principle #1:

The first command from God to man is of prosperity. God's number one desire for you is all round prosperity. Open up

your mind and spirit as you continue to read for ideas on what to do in order to become a millionaire. I assure you God will begin to drop divine ideas into your spirit.

Genesis 1:27- 28, *"So God created man in His own image; in the image of God He created him; male and female He created them. Then God blessed them, and said to them "Be fruitful and multiply, fill the earth and subdue it. Have dominion over the fish of the sea, over the birds of the air, and over every living thing that moves on the earth"*.

Here are some Ideas on what you can do to become a millionaire.

The first command from God to man is one of prosperity, but when the first Adam fell man lost that blessing. However, when the last Adam, Jesus Christ, came man regained the blessing.

In other words, the moment you begin to seek first the kingdom of God and His righteousness every other thing shall be added unto you.

Your right to prosperity which you lost initially will be added back unto you. You will begin to be fruitful, and you will start to multiply in the works of your hands.

The bible says in Deuteronomy 30:9 *"Then the Lord your God will make you most **prosperous** in all the work of your hands and in the fruit of your womb, the young of your livestock and the crops of your land. The Lord will again delight in you and make you **prosperous**, just as he delighted in your fathers"*.

- ☐ It means that you will begin to produce your own products and start making some serious money.
- ☐ You will start re-investing your money in your products and in other businesses.
- ☐ You will begin to buy organisations.
- ☐ You will establish co-operations.
- ☐ You will build houses and rent them out to people with housing problems and many more.

And because God has made you a millionaire you will use some of the money for good and Godly causes.

Let us pray:

Father Lord in heaven, I pray that as your son or daughter continues to listen to you and practise your principles as detailed in your word and this book, you will do what only You God can do in his or her life in Jesus name. Amen.

Hint: - Continuous income is when you do something once and it continues to bring in money. Think of something that you only need to do once and the money would continues to flow forever, and begin to do it from today. Do not wait till tomorrow before you start, because if you do, the spirit of procrastination will never allow tomorrow to come. Procrastination is an enemy to prosperity.

It is time to study another scripture:

Scripture five in support of principle #1

2nd Chronicles 26:5 "*He sought God in the days of Zechariah, who had understanding in the visions of God; and as long as he sought the Lord, God made him prosper*".

Prophetic words from the prophetess under the anointing of God:

My beloved, "I prophesy into your life that as you continue to read this book, you will receive supernatural grace to seek God first daily in your life. As you do so, the strength to hear and obey Him will come to you regarding all the affairs of life.

You will start to desire and apply His will into every situation of life and God will make you prosper. He will give you ideas that will elevate you into a new level.

God says it in the above scripture believe it and it shall come to pass in your life. You will prosper! You shall prosper!! There is no doubt about it!!! It is your birth right to prosper as a child of God who seeks him daily. The bible says "your beginnings will seem humble, so **prosperous** will your future be" -Job 8:7.

Confess the following prayers:

Now that I have understood what God says about my prosperity I have made up my mind to follow His ways. In all my ways I will acknowledge you O Lord and I know that you will direct my path. I confess that I am prosperous.

I decree prosperity upon my life and that of my family in Jesus name. Amen.

Hint: - A one off income is when you only get paid once for your effort. This is not a good way to leverage your effort. You need the best and the smartest way to become a millionaire. In actual fact, the sooner you make your way to becoming a millionaire the better, so that you can enjoy your money longer. Cultivate the habit of sitting down quietly on your own in a quiet area for at least an hour every day and ask yourself some really good questions about becoming financially free. It will amaze you the type of answers you are able to unveil.

Let us look into the next scripture and see what we can learn from it.

Scripture six in support of principle #1:

Understand the pleasure of the Lord through seeking Him first and you will make money.

"Yet it pleased the Lord to bruise Him; He has put Him to grief. When you made His soul an offering for sin, He shall see His seed, He shall prolong His days, and the pleasure of the Lord shall prosper in His hand" - Isaiah 53:10

Work with God and become a millionaire.

This is where we are *going "and the pleasure of God shall prosper in his hand"*.

My beloved brothers and sisters, I want you to grasp this in your spirit. When you begin to seek first the kingdom of God and his righteousness, you will understand His pleasure and you will begin to apply it to every situation in your life including your financial situation.

Then God shall prosper you and everything you lay your hands on from that moment henceforth will blossom. God says in Psalm 1:3, "*He is like a tree planted by streams of water, which yields its fruit in season and whose leaf does not wither. Whatever he does prospers.* This is your testimony in Christ, in Jesus name".

Every tongue that rises up against you in judgement shall be condemned in Jesus name. Amen.

God will open up your understanding to prosperity.

As God begins to prosper you in your financial dealings, He will open up your understanding about you owning your own businesses.

- ☐ God will show you how to have your own organizational companies.
- ☐ He will show you how to become a dimensionalist.

☐ He will also show you how to solve people's problems and you will become a millionaire as you continue to walk with Him.

Hint: Remember Investment! Investment!! Investment!!! You must start a regular investment. This is your best way to becoming a millionaire. It is the best way to leverage your money.

Let's study the last scripture on this principle.

Scripture seven on principle #1:

Divine assurance that you can become a millionaire:

Isaiah 55:11,-"*So shall my word be that goes forth from my mouth; it shall not return to me void, but it shall accomplish what I please, and it shall prosper in the things for which I sent it*".

You will prosper

Since the word of God says seek first the kingdom of God, and you have obeyed him and sought him first, you have done what God asked you to do, therefore his word will not return empty in your life.

Rather, it shall accomplish what He pleases and therefore you have prospered and have become very prosperous. You are made rich in Christ. You are moneyed, which means you are wealthy, affluent, prosperous, well to do and rich. You are a creator of wealth. That is your portion in Jesus name.

Every disease in your body will flee and healing will replace it because you must prosper. Prosperity in Christ is all around you. This includes health, peace, joy and family blessings.

I decree over your life that "every financial block be removed and financial favours come your way and you become a millionaire because you must prosper in Jesus name".

Every depression must flee and happiness will replace it because you must prosper.

I have come to let you know that because my Lord Jesus Christ cannot come in person He has sent me. He said "I should tell you that because you have obeyed him you will prosper! You shall prosper!! You must prosper!!! Hallelujah! Glory"

At this point you need to say another prayer for yourself:

My father in Heaven, I know that you have put your power in my tongue. I use that power to release your blessings and prosperity upon my life.

I pray that I will always recognise your presence through your still small voice. I know by faith that as I use the power in my tongue to create my heaven on earth you will continue to prosper me in all I lay my hands to do in Jesus name. Amen.

Hint: - Making money is like a game. Knowing how to play it will enable you to win and make some serious money to the glory of God. However, if you don't know how to play the game of money you might remain under the bondage of finance for a long time, sometimes it could be for a lifetime. The good news is that the game of making money can be learnt. You need to look for somebody who has what you wanted and offer to work for them. Offer to help them, even if you have to do it for free, do it, it's only for a period of time, and you will be glad you helped with your time because it will pay off in future, like Elisha for Elijah and the disciples for Jesus.

CHAPTER TWO

Principle #2: you must be willing to be obedient to God's word

In this chapter I am going to teach the second principle you need to hold onto in order to become a millionaire:

The second principle you need to apply in order to become a millionaire is:

Be Obedient to the word of a man of God or a woman of God.

This is because sometimes God will send his word through his servants to you. The bible clearly says your prosperity is in the hand of the prophet. *"**Believe in the Lord your God, so shall you be established, believe his prophets, so shall you prosper**"* - 2nd chronicles 20:20.

Why must I be obedient to the word of God and how does this apply to my prosperity and my becoming a millionaire?

Let us study the first Scripture on this principle.

Scripture one in support of principle #2:

Isaiah 1:19 the word of God says *"if you are willing and obedient, you shall eat the good of the land"*.

Poverty shall have no place in your life and the lives of your generations.

God is saying that if you will read His word, understand and obey Him by applying His principles to your situation then you will discover the wisdom you need to solve your problems and you will be able to eat the good of the land.

In other words, God is saying that you will have good health because it is the good of the land, no disease shall befall you because that is not the good of the land.

He says you will have many businesses because it is the good of the land.

God says you will prosper and became a millionaire because that is the good of the land. Poverty shall have no place in your life because that is not the good of the land.

Reduction shall have no place in your life because it is not the good of the land, instead increases will begin to have a place in you because it is the good of the land.

Bareness will not have a place in your life because it is not the good of the land. Rather, you will give birth to as many children as you want because it is the good of the land.

Remember it is your birthright to eat the good of the land once you obey God.

My prayer for you:

My prayer for you is that you will eat all the good of the land and whatever is not good on the land will run away from you and evil will never be your portion in Jesus name, Amen.

Hint: - You need a portfolio of income flow. I mean many sources of income flow, not one not even two. In other words you need to put many products of yours in the market world.

We need to be obedient to faith in order to have the wisdom to become a millionaire.

What is this second scripture trying to tell you? Well let us find out.

Scripture two in support of principle #2:

Act 6:7 *"then the word of God spread, and the number of the disciples multiplied greatly in Jerusalem, and a great many of the priests were obedient to the faith.*

God will expose the work of the enemy to you once you choose to walk in obedience to His word.

My beloved, I pray that as you read God's words, your lives will change for good. You will begin to see the light and through seeing the light, the work of the enemy will be exposed to you.

You will be obedient to faith which will give you wisdom and understanding about the will of God regarding your prosperity.

It will also expose you to the will of God regarding the transformation and reformation that you need to put in place so that you can move from where you are right now in your financial situation, to where God has ordained for you to be; such as becoming a millionaire and using some of the money to sponsor the gospel.

I want to let you know that as you continue to sponsor the Gospel, your money will continue to multiply a hundred fold and in no time a thousand fold and you will soon become a multi-millionaire.

As a prophetess of God, the Lord Jesus Christ said I should tell you that God is delighted in you becoming a multi-millionaire in a way that is dignifying to God the Father. And my prayer

Is that you will get there in Jesus name, Amen.

Rich words of advice on becoming a millionaire

Lean forward today and begin to posses your possession by doing the following.

☐ Start your own businesses.

☐ Become a real estate owner.

☐ Invest in high interest funds.

☐ Have your own financial houses in other words open your own (Banks).

☐ Start buying off organisation that are failing and reinstate them.

☐ Become an employer not an employee.

☐ You need to determine and make up your mind that you want to be above only and no more beneath, head only and no more the tail.

☐ You need to become a distribution centre, no more a poor person begging for bread. (Bread here does not mean a loaf of bread but every good thing of life which you need to have).

Prayer:

I pray that God will make a way for you where others are finding it difficult to breakthrough and you will be able to achieve most of the above if not all of them in Jesus name.

Hint: - Real estate is a good and quick route to becoming a millionaire. Start buying houses today and rent them out to people with housing problems, they will be happy to pay you weekly or monthly depending on whichever arrangement is convenient for you and your customers.

God will remember his covenant with your fore father Abraham when you begin to obey Him and He will make you a millionaire.

Scripture three on principle #2:

Deuteronomy 5:30-31 *"when you are distressed and all these things come upon you in latter days when you turn to the Lord your God and obey His voice; for the Lord your God is a merciful God, He will not forsake you nor destroy you, nor forget the covenant of your fathers which he swore to them".*

God is about to turn your tears into laughter

In other words, this means God can turn people's tears into Joy when they start to obey Him.

He can turn hopeless situations into something meaningful. God can turn a mess into a message once you begin to obey His word.

Ladies and Gentlemen, if your financial situation is in a mess change your principles, start obeying God's word and suddenly you will see him turn your situation around.

He will give you the wisdom and ability to start your own businesses and some investment and in no time He will prosper the work of your hands. God is pleased to bless you with many skills.

He will remember the covenant of blessing which He has made with your father Abraham and He will bless you even beyond your wildest imagination and you will become a multi-millionaire.

Hint: - Good marketing of your products are ways of letting people know about what you are doing. Remember, the more people know about your product, the more they will patronize you and the quicker you will become a millionaire. Therefore make marketing of your product a priority.

God is a jealous God. He doesn't want you to worship any other god except Him.

Scripture four on principle #2:

Now therefore *"he said put away the foreign gods which are among you and incline your heart to the Lord God of Israel." And the people said to Joshua, "The Lord our God we will serve and His voice we will obey!"*- Joshua 24:23-24

The result of the people's actions to serve God and to obey only His voice was tremendous. Following their action, God blessed these people beyond their imagination.

God just loves to bless you with a lot of money

My beloved, please obey the Voice of God and allow your joy to be full. Focus on Him alone and put no other gods beside Him. Remember, God said that He is a jealous God. Therefore, do not put your trust in any other thing but God.

If you have done this, then you have obeyed Him and have put yourself in the position to be blessed. Then God has no option but to bless you with good health, children, peace, joy, and salvation for your whole household.

And of course He will also bless you with a lot of money that you can not finish spending in your life time but will leave for your children's children.

My sister and brother in the Lord, it is my desire that you prosper. And as long as my God reigns, you will prosper in every good thing that you lay your hands to do in Jesus name. Amen.

Pray for yourself:

My father in heaven I recognised your presence here as I am reading this book.

I pray that my life and the lives of my families will never be the same again after I finish reading this book in Jesus name. Amen.

Hint: - A small and good business anointed by God can turn you into a millionaire in no time. Make God the Managing director of your businesses. Ask the Holy Spirit to direct you before you transact any business with anybody however small the business may be.

Obey God and not a man as you are becoming a millionaire.

Scripture five on principle #2:

Acts 5:29 - The Bible says "Peter and the other apostles answered and said "We ought to obey God rather than men".

Peter and the apostles recognized the true God who needs to be worshiped and obeyed. They knew that we should not obey men but God.

Appreciate the professional judgement of the medical doctors but obey God's voice.

My beloved, whose voice do you obey in your life?

I appreciate the doctors greatly and I respect their professional judgement.

But when the doctors say to you that you have cancer, which cannot be cured and that you have only a few month or days to live on earth how do you express your faith?

Do you just believe what they say and start awaiting death to come and take you home? Or do you say, it aloud through your mouth, although I appreciate medical diagnosis, I believe in the word of God that says at the name of Jesus every sicknesses and diseases will flee.

My beloved, I brought you the good news that as you begin to obey God's voice, diseases and sicknesses will be a thing of the past in your life.

Poverty will be replaced with wealth, prosperity, and of course with a lot of money and many blessings that God has in stock for you. Amen.

Now it is time to pray:

Father in heaven I praise and adore you, since I am your child, I will continue to listen to you; I pray that you should continue to fulfil all your promises in my life in Jesus name. Amen.

Hint: - Make most of your income a continuous income so that you can enjoy **Time Freedom.**

You must be able to obey God by faith on your way to becoming a millionaire.

Scripture six on principle #2:

Hebrews 11:8, "*by faith Abraham obeyed when he was called to go out to the place which he would receive as an inheritance. And he went out not knowing where he was going*".

You must step forward and start your business by faith

God loves you and when you obey Him by faith there is nothing he cannot do for you. Just say to Him "father you are able and here I am, bless me" I believe if you can do it for Abraham you are able to do much more for me. If Abraham had not obeyed God by faith he would have missed all his blessings. Therefore go a step further today, determine to change your life and that of your generations. Obey God by faith. You should start your own business right now.

When you begin to sense it in your spirit that God wants you to go and start your business, take that step of faith and start the business with no doubt in your mind. Money or no money, Faith is all you need, because your faith can produce for you any thing you desire.

And when you have obeyed God and started the business, He will make it happen for you. He will cause it to flourish in Jesus name.

You will need to carry out some research in order for you to know what you are doing, but you must step forward and start. And as you take this giant step, my prayer is that God will start to bless you financially until you become exceedingly prosperous in Jesus name.

My beloved, as a prophetess, pastor and the servant of the Lord Jesus Christ, I was sent to bring you this good news that God has already blessed you abundantly.

Begin to use your faith, and once you obey God by faith He will start to manifest that blessing through you. The impossibilities will become possible for your sake.

Remember to make long term financial plans which include long term goals, and a long term review. Refuse to spend money on stuff that aren't important. Believe me beloved you will make it.

Now pray:

My father in heaven, with faith in my heart I pray the following prayer in the name of Jesus Christ. I believe in my heart and spirit that you are able to answer my prayers and make them come to pass in my life.

☐ I pray that from this moment henceforth I will receive my breakthrough.

- ☐ I bind and I disgrace every sorrow in my life.
- ☐ Lord Jesus, let miracle burst forth in my life right now.
- ☐ You spirit of procrastination I bind you in Jesus name
- ☐ You wicked spirit of death I cast you out because I will not die before the manifestation of my miracles in Jesus name
- ☐ O Lord Jesus I believe that you are the Lord of suddenly. Manifest the miracle of suddenly in my life in Jesus name I have prayed. Amen.

Hint: - Examples of Continuous income are real estate and investments into mutual funds. Remember, do not wait for an opportunity to become a millionaire, instead, create one for yourself, and begin to enjoy a wealthy lifestyle.

There is a reward attached to being humble and obedient:

Scripture seven to support principle #2

Philippians 2:8 – 11, "*being found in appearance as man, He humbled Himself and became obedient to the point of death, even the death of the cross. Therefore God also has highly exalted Him and given Him the name which is above every name, that at the name of Jesus every knee should bow, of those in heaven, and of those on earth, and those under the earth, and that every tongue should confess that Jesus Christ is Lord to the glory of God the Father*".

You will not only become a millionaire but a multi-millionaire

Beloved, I sincerely oblige you to be obedient to God and His words through reading of the bible and applying the biblical principles to your life.

I believe that God will change your life not only for the better, but for the best. You will not only become a millionaire but a multi- millionaire.

Because you are obedient to Him, your obedience will automatically open the floodgates of heaven for you, and ideas that you will need to turn into products will begin to flow into your minds.

Therefore as you begin to turn these ideas into products, people will begin to buy them, and money will start flowing into your bank accounts, and this will turn you into a multi-millionaire.

My beloved, see you on your way to becoming a millionaire, and by the grace of God you will make it.

CHAPTER THREE

Principle #3: You must be willing to be Righteous.

The Lord loves the righteous and he will give them the desire of their heart.

Scripture one to support principle #3:

Psalm 146: 8 "*The Lord opens the eyes of the blind; The Lord raises those who are bowed down; The Lord loves the righteous*".

Beloved, take the decision to be righteous today, and automatically begin to enjoy the fruit of righteousness.

Hint: Your destiny is in your hands. Start taking actions that will propel you to becoming a multi-millionaire from today. It is either of two things in life. It is either you start acting and begin to experience prosperity which is the reward of action or you don't act and nothing changes.

God will provide you with giant ideas that will bring money to you in the range of millions.

In other words the fact that you are righteous means the Lord loves you and has made you His beloved child. He will guide you and protect you. You will never fail or lose out.

God will bless you with your own children. He will rejoice over you as a child of the Kingdom of Heaven.

- ☐ He will provide you with money to look after your children.
- ☐ He will give you money to sponsor the Gospel.
- ☐ He will give you money to care for the needy.
- ☐ He will provide you with money to sponsor the motherless children.
- ☐ He will give you money to feed, clothe and educate the orphans.
- ☐ He will provide you with money in abundance to build hospitals where the sick can receive health.

Definitely, the money needed in order to achieve all the above things are in the range of multi-millions and that is the reason why God will provide you with giant ideas that will provide money in the range of millions so that you can bring glory to his name.

Hint: - Remember to cultivate the habit of saving at least 20% of your gross monthly income. A continuous monthly investment over a period of time is bound to accumulate to something reasonable which you can use to start a money generating project.

God will bless the righteous with everything including money and making you a millionaire

Scripture two to support principle #3:

Psalm 5:12 *"for You O Lord, will bless the righteous"*.

The right people to make your dream become a reality will come your way.

Child of God, do you know that the Lord has promised to bless the righteous? Do you know that God said in his word that heaven and earth will pass away but none of His words shall go unaccomplished?

Do you know that God cannot lie? The fact that He said He will bless the righteous means that He will bless you once you are righteous.

Child of the Most High, God said I should tell you that He will bless you abundantly the moment you begin to have a passion for righteousness.

He said He will send you the right people that will help you to make your financial dreams come to pass. The Lord will send you people that are able and willing to give you the information you need to know for you to start your own business. This same people will show you where to get all the help you need to progress and succeed in all your endeavours.

Hint: - You need automated investing plan. This is where you invest regularly regardless of whether the market is up, down or sideways. A long term investment will help you become what God wants you to become.

O God, my heavenly father, I pray that you and you alone should bless me and make my desire to become a millionaire come to pass in Jesus name. Amen.

God acknowledges the ways of the righteous as he or she is trying to become a dignified millionaire.

Scripture three to support principle #3:

Psalm 1:5-6 *"therefore the ungodly shall not stand in the judgement, or the sinners in the congregation of the righteous. For the Lord knows the way of the righteous"*.

You will achieve your purposes in all aspects of life and you will become a millionaire.

The Bible says that the Lord knows the way of the righteous. Because God knows your ways due to your righteousness, your way to accomplish your financial freedom shall be made clear to you.

And also, for that reason the devil is a looser in your life. Do you know that the Holy Spirit has been living in the inside of you since the moment you confessed and declared the Lord Jesus Christ as your Lord and personal saviour?

The fact that the one leaving in the inside of you is greater than the one in the world automatically made you a winner over the devil and the spirit of fear. Therefore be glad and continue to rejoice because this battle is already won on your behalf.

REFLECTION TIME

Take a minute to reflect on what you have learnt.

Well done you are truly going to become a millionaire as that is the desire of your heart.

God bless.

You shall not perish, but succeed in every good thing you do. You will achieve your dreams and purposes in all aspects of life. God I beg you to grant me peace of mind in life in Jesus name. You will be fruitful because you will produce your own products. God is faithful to you. You will be able to solve other   people's problems and the reward of solving problems is money.

As a prophetess of the Lord Jesus "I prophesy into your life that you will have money beyond your widest imagination. Your dreams shall not die. Your wealth will become your strong city. You will achieve all your desires and dreams and will breakthrough from all angles in Jesus name. Amen".

Pray for yourself:

- ☐ I pray that every anti success demon in my life be consumed by the fire of the Holy Ghost.
- ☐ I command the oppressors to vomit all my progress which they have swallowed in Jesus name.
- ☐ God thank you for fighting my battles in Jesus name.
- ☐ I command every evil spirit oppressing me to lose their hold and burn into ashes in Jesus name. Amen.
- ☐ I protect my dream with the blood of Jesus.

Hint: - You need an outstanding product or service of your own out there in the marketplace. Ask yourself this question aloud; what product of mine is out there in the marketplace that whenever some body buys it I become richer? If your answer to this question is "none" then you need to start diverting all your energy towards making a product.

Your becoming a millionaire is your strong city

Scripture four to support principle #3

Proverbs 10:15 - 17 *"the rich man's wealth is his strong city; the destruction of the poor is their poverty. The labour of the righteous lead to life, while the wages of the wicked to sin. He who keeps instruction is in the way of life, but he who refuses correction goes astray.*

Prayer:

I like to join hands with you in the spirit and pray in agreement that the Lord Jesus Christ will make you rich because it is your birthright to be rich. The bible says in 2nd Corinthians 8:9, *"For you know the grace of our Lord Jesus Christ, that though he was rich, yet for your sakes he became poor, so that you through his poverty might become rich". Jesus has paid for your poverty.* You will never be poor in your life in Jesus name.

Since the rich man's wealth is his strong city, I pray that from this moment henceforth you will not taste poverty anymore in your life. The Bible says the destruction of the poor is their poverty and God does not want to destroy you since you are one of His righteous children.

The good news to you from our Lord Jesus Christ

I bring the good news to you from our Lord Jesus that because you have the passion for righteousness and you have determined to be righteous and not wicked, God is watching over you.

Now that you are actually practising righteousness, it means you are keeping Gods word in all your ways of life. Therefore, you will never go astray but goodness and mercy will follow you all the days of your life in Jesus name, Amen.

For this reason, the Lord God of Abraham, Isaac and Jacob will prosper your ways. He will bless you with money. God loves you to have millions and be a blessing to many. His desire for you is to own companies, organisation, toy manufacturing companies, petrol stations and many more of your own.

God wants you to own the best of everything he created and make some serious money. He knows that whatever blessing he entrusts into your hands will be used wisely to bring Him glory. You are already blessed. You are already RICH. Speak it out of your mouth in faith and you will become it. Say it now "I am a Millionaire". That is your portion in Jesus name.

Hint: - Your continuous income needs to be continual even when you are not present. Continuous income such as income from real estate does not need your presence for it to continue growing.

Another benefit of being righteous is that your descendant will never lack anything or beg for bread. In your life, you will make millions that you cannot finish spending in your lifetime. This blessing will continue to your tenth generations:

Scripture five to support principle #3:

Psalm 37:25 - 26 *"I have been young, and now am old; yet I have not seen the righteous forsaken, nor his descendants begging bread. He is ever merciful, and lends; and his descendant are blessed"*.

Money generating machine for you

Because you are a righteous person God will never forsake you, neither will your descendant ever beg for bread.

Listen to this my beloved, the moment you begin to be righteous you have placed yourself in the position for God to be merciful to you. Do you know that once God is merciful to you, disease, poverty and depression will become a thing of the past in your life?

Bareness, unhappiness and fear will all become a thing of the past. God will begin to replace all your lack with plenty. He will heal all your diseases.

He will give you plenty of money to replace the poverty you have ever experience in your life. God will turn your depression into a passion for a divine idea. He will confer and bestow an individualised idea for you. God will give you an uncommon idea, which is personally packaged for you with your name written on it by Jesus.

You will be able to turn this idea into a product which will solve other people's problems and this will become a money generating machine for you. It will generate billions of pounds into your bank accounts.

You will leave an inheritance for your children's children

God also promised in the above scripture that your descendant will be blessed. God will bless you with billions and billions of pounds in your bank account. You will live up to a ripe age and leave an inheritance for your children's children in Jesus name. Amen.

Hint: - You need to identify a problem and start solving it. There are a million and one problem in the world today awaiting solutions. Look carefully around you today. I'm sure you will be able to identify an area where you can be of help, create a passion for this area and in no time people will be willing to pay you for your energy.

Your hope as a righteous person is gladness

Scripture Six to support principle #3:

Proverbs 10:28 "*the hope of the righteous will be gladness, but the expectation of the wicked will perish*".

You will give birth to children until you are satisfied and want no more.

Child of the Most High God, Jesus said I should tell you that once you are righteous all your hopelessness will be turned to hope. And the sadness in your home will be turned to gladness.

The wayward child will return home and will begin to serve God and this will gladden your heart. Regarding your business, God said your heart will be gladdened. Your competitors and customers will find gladness in your goods and services, because of the anointing of God upon your life.

In your spouse you will find joy and gladness. My sister, in your womb you will find gladness because you will give birth to healthy children until you are satisfied.

You will own organisations and corporations

In all your business endeavours you will make plenty of money and your heart will be gladdened. You will buy businesses that will make you prosper.

Whatever you lay your hands to do will prosper.

You will own organisations and corporations that will make billions of money. Remember, you are entitled to own real estates and properties that will generate money for you twenty four hours a day for the rest of your life.

The devourer will be rebuked for your sake. You will lend money to many nations but will not borrow. God will not allow you to lack any good thing in Jesus Name.

Every day of your life you will find purposes and fulfilments and therefore you will rejoice and be glad.

Hint: - A good and continuous income includes when you become a software creator.

Remember, if you do not create your own products you will have nothing to sell and if there is nothing for you to sell, there will be no money coming into your bank account from the market place.

Beloved, creating software is a product, so also is hosting web-sites. Think about it and start something today. So that when you look back in a few years time from now you will be glad you did something. You will be glad that you took that step of faith.

Because you are righteous, your businesses will flourish and you will become a millionaire:

Scripture seven to support principle #3:

Proverbs 11:28 "*He who trusts in his riches will fall. But the righteous will flourish like foliage.*

The following are Inspirations from the Holy Spirit under the anointing of the Holy Ghost.

My brother and sister in Christ, once you follow the principles in this book you will prosper as we have discussed earlier on.

You will be rich even beyond your wildest imagination. There is no doubt about it because everything written in this book was inspired under the anointing of the Holy Spirit. I am convinced in my spirit beyond reasonable doubt that as you obey and do what God says you will become a multi-millionaire.

Jesus sounded it audibly in my spirit that I should let you know that when the time comes and you have become a millionaire, God said He wants you to remain humble and not trust in your riches so that you will continue to grow wealthy.

He said a man who trusts in his riches will fall!

Instead of trusting in your riches, Jesus said you should be righteous so that you will flourish like foliage.

Hint: - Another good and continuous income is you becoming an actor or an actress.

CHAPTER FOUR

Principle #4: You must be willing to promote the truth and build your trust in the God of truth.

The Lord Jesus Christ is the God of truth. Build your trust in Him and He will guide you until you become a millionaire.

Scripture one to support principle #4:

Deuteronomy 32:4 says *"He is the Rock His work is perfect; for all His ways are justice. A God of truth and without injustice; righteous and upright is He"*.

Your life will take on a different dimension which will lead you to becoming a millionaire.

The bible says that God is the Rock. He is a God of truth and without injustice.

Beloved, how would you like to build your trust in this type of God, who is a God of truth? He is a great God, He is Mighty.

I'm presenting to you the God of Jacob, and the God of Isaac. He is the God we are talking about here today. Brethren, this is the God that answers by fire, He is my God and yours too.

I personally would not like to build my trust on a false god and I am sure you will not too.

Therefore build your trust in this God that the bible is telling you about and see miracles spring up in your life.

Do you know that everything in His word is truth? Do you know that the bible says this God does not lie?

For these reasons I believed that as you begin to put your trust in Him by reading His word, believing in it, and putting it to practise, your life will take on a different dimension and will never be the same again.

As you do these, all the road blocks on your way to having your own children will be removed.

God said all the road blocks standing in the way of you finding your own life partner will be removed In Jesus Name.

Beloved, the stumbling block in the way of your financial breakthrough will become a history. Finally, all those Jericho walls built against you shall come down one after the other in Jesus name. Amen.

Rich words of advice.

Once the road blocks are removed, financially you will begin to see and think clearly. Your reasoning ability will make sense to you. You will begin to see a clearer vision. You will be empowered to reach forward and take meaningful actions that will propel you to your greatness. You will take actions that will make you take decisions to start your own businesses.

You will be able to take actions that will enable you to start your own real estate business. You will take actions that will make you buy your own petroleum companies.

☐ Become a distributor of cars.
☐ Start manufacturing different products.
☐ Start a multi level marketing business and many more.

My prayer for you is that you will not miss vital opportunities any more in your life in Jesus name.

Hint: - Keep your housing expenses to 25% of your gross continuous income.

Scripture two to support principle #4:

Every single promise of God to you, including the one for your prosperity will come to pass.

God is not a man so He does not lie, "The word of God says in Isaiah 55:10-11 *"For as the rain comes down and the snow from heavens, and do not return there but waters the earth, and make it bring forth and bud, that it may give seed to the sower and bread to the eater, so shall My word be that goes forth from My mouth; it shall not return to me void, but it shall accomplish what I please, and it shall prosper in the thing for which I sent it".*

My beloved, believe in God's words and you will receive all the blessings he has for you then you will be able to open your mouth and proclaim that your God is good and his mercies endure forever.

Hint: - Cultivate a business person's mindset. Think and pray regularly for business ideas that can move you forward to a higher level. Pray for ideas that can make you a millionaire and give you financial freedom for the rest of your life.

You must speak the truth in your heart.

Scripture three in support of principle #4:

- Psalm 15:1-2 "*Lord who may abide in your tabernacle? Who may dwell in your holy hill? He who is upright, works righteousness, and speaks the truth in his heart*".
- Money in abundance will become your lot.

Beloved, once you have promoted the truth in your heart and you have made the God of truth your God, you will be able to abide in the Lord's tabernacle, and you will be able to dwell in His holy hill.

The moment you begin to dwell in God's holy hill, sickness and disease will flee from you. Bareness will flee from you. Unrighteousness will flee from you. Poverty will also flee from you. Money in abundance will become your lot and you will never lack again.

Hint: - Working for somebody will never make you a millionaire, but the determination to work for yourself and acting on the determination will make you rich and put money in your pocket.

Trust God with all your undertakings while you are on your way to making your millions and mercy shall surround you all the way through.

Scripture four to support principle #4:

Psalm 32:10 - 11 *"Many sorrows shall be to the wicked; but he who trusts in the Lord, mercy shall surround him. Be glad in the Lord and rejoice, you upright in heart!*

Mercy will pave ways for you until you become a millionaire.

Whosoever trusts in the Lord will not have sorrow but mercy shall surround him. Mercy will pave way for you until you prosper and you begin to make some serious money.

Mercy will make a way for you until you have your own businesses. I say mercy will pave ways for you until help starts running towards you and over takes you. People will hear your voice on the phone and they will help and favour you.

People who do not know you will only hear about you and what you are doing and they will help you. People will see your signature and they will help you. People will see what belongs to you and they will help you. All the above are things that you will experience the moment mercy begin to work with you.

Beloved, God is real. Jesus Christ is alive and the Holy Sprit is wonderful.

Put your trust in God and you will not experience lack any longer.

Hint: - You need a long term regular investment.

It is important for you not to lean on your own understanding but to acknowledge God because you need Him to direct your path towards your journey to becoming a millionaire.

Scripture five to support principle #4:

Proverbs 3:5-6 *"trust in the Lord with all your heart, and lean not on your own understanding; in all your ways acknowledge Him, and He shall direct your paths"*.

A message from the Lord Jesus Christ

My brother and sister in Christ, Jesus sent me to tell you "that as you continue to trust in the Lord with all your heart' and stop leaning on your own understanding, God will make it His responsibility to bless you and make you prosper".

"He will send men and women your way to come and take you, by hand, to the land full of gold and silver".

He said he will send you people who will go out of their way to show you how to make money in a way that is dignifying to God. God will bless you and make you a blessing to others. God will lay in your heart which investment you should put your money in that will give you a very high return. He will teach you how to put your money into real estate. He will show you what businesses to start, and which companies and corporations you can own.

God will teach you regarding which franchise you should put your money in. Once God is the one showing you all these things, you can never go wrong. Rather your millions will continue to multiply until you become a multi-millionaire and then progress to a billionaire. Then you will continue to help the widow, the motherless, the poor and less fortunate people and your billions will continue to multiply more and more until you want no more.

God will direct your path

Now that you have started to acknowledge God in all your ways, He promised to direct your path. Once God is the one directing your path, you can never fail but instead you will continue to be fruitful in all that you lay your hands on to do in Jesus name. Amen.

Prayer points:

- ☐ Now that I know the truth, I command every manipulating spirit in my life to be bound with fetters of iron in Jesus name. Amen.

- ☐ I release the fire of the Holy Spirit to burn outright every demonic entity blocking my prosperity and my way to becoming a millionaire in Jesus Name.

- ☐ Every stubborn spirit planning to trouble me on my way to becoming a millionaire I bind you in the name of Jesus.

- ☐ You wicked spirit of anti millionaire I crush your head in Jesus name.

- ☐ I will not be a failure in Jesus name.

- ☐ I have set out my goal and have planed to become a millionaire. I will achieve my goal very soon in Jesus name.

Hint: - Start your own business. There are a lot of business opportunities and ideas out there. Look into one of them and research deeply into it and start turning it into money.

You need the Lord Jesus Christ in your life:

Scripture six to support principle #4

John 14:6 Jesus said "*I am the way, the truth, and the life. No one comes to the Father except through Me*".

Poverty is a curse so it is not your portion.

Beloved, since Jesus Christ revealed Himself as the truth, the light and the life, let us trust Him and see all the good results in our lives. Let his light lead you and guide you. Refuse to work in darkness.

One thing I know and which is very clear to me is that you can not put all your trust in the Lord and still be poor, No WAY, it is impossible.

Poverty is a curse. It then becomes a thing of the past in your life because darkness and light can never mix.

You will make your money in a very big and advanced way. You will make it in a way that will not put the name of the Lord to shame.

Hint: - You must have the desire to become a millionaire and do everything within your reach to achieve that desire.

You do not need to be afraid on your way to making your cool money therefore make God your salvation.

Scripture seven to support principle #4:

Isaiah 12:2, "*Behold, God is my salvation, I will trust and not be afraid; for YAH, the Lord, is my strength and song; He also has become my salvation.*

Fear is not your portion it is from the devil.

My beloved, may I bring it to your notice that once you have your total trust in God, you must not be afraid because He will take care of your past, present and future.

As a prophetess of God, Jesus said I should tell you that the future is bright. He said this is because eyes have not seen and ears have not heard, neither has it come to the mind of men what God has in stock for your future.

Therefore you should begin to rejoice and begin to thank God because you are already on your way to becoming a multi millionaire. Your dreams and imaginations are about to come into reality. It is about to come to past. Your eyes will see it and your hands will handle it in Jesus name.

Psalm 91:4-5 "*He shall cover you with His feathers, and under His wings you shall take refuge; His truth shall be your shield and buckler.*

You must not stay too long on a **JOB** because it means just over broke.

The Lord said I should bring you this good news. That once you begin to read His word and believe in it and put it into practise then you have found the truth and that truth shall be your shield and buckler.

God said he will cover you with His feathers and under his wings you shall take refuge. Beloved and chosen one of God, God is real and Jesus Christ is alive. God will manifest His power in your businesses and in your job.

Although you need to have your own business, and not just working for an employer forever, but you can use your present job as your conveyance vehicle to investing in your own businesses. It is a good starting point.

You must not stay too long on a JOB because it means Just OVER Broke. A JOB can never make you rich.

You can only become a millionaire by owning your own businesses.

My brothers and sisters, do not be afraid. God will show you how to become an entrepreneur. He will show you how to make money flow to you like a river. You are already blessed in Jesus name.

CHAPTER FIVE

Principle #5: You must be willing to watch your tongue, speak no evil about yourself or others and Keep your lips from speaking deceit.

If you want to see the goodness of God in your life, you must be prepared to refrain your tongue from speaking evil so that God can prosper you and make you a millionaire.

Scripture one in support of principle #5:

Psalm 34:11-14, *"Come you children listen to me, I will teach you the fear of the Lord. Who is the man who desires life, and loves many days, that he may see good? Keep your tongue from evil and your lips from speaking deceit".*

There is power in the tongue

My beloved, do you know that there is power in the tongue? Do you know that it is very important for you to always confess positively? Do you know that whatsoever you bind on earth is bound in heaven and whatsoever you loose on earth is loosed in heaven?

Beloved, I beg you in the name which is above all names, the name of our Lord Jesus Christ that you should be careful with your tongue.

Wonderful child of the Most High, God is about to do what only He can do in your life!

Repeat these words of affirmation.

I want you to repeat this statement aloud three times as you are reading this book, (Put your name) "I am blessed with wisdom and I am establishing different types of businesses. I am establishing different types of organisations, and different types of franchises. I am capable of having different types of manufacturing companies which are producing thousands of different products to bless the world and make me a millionaire".

I am a dimensionalist. I am solving people's problems in different dimensions and as money is the reward of solving problems, money is running to me in thousands, in millions, and also in billions In Jesus name.

I can do it. Others have done it in the past I will do it and achieve all that I have written down in my plans to achieve.

Hint: - Believe in yourself that you can handle businesses that will produce billions of dollars and you will see what you believe manifest itself in your life.

You need to guard your tongue at all times.

Scripture two in support of principle #5:

Psalm 39-1 *"I said I will guard my ways, less I sin with my tongue; I will restrain my mouth with a muzzle, while the wicked are before me.*

Thinking and speaking positively are the things that will help you become a millionaire and also enable you to get every other thing you require in this life.

The bible says *"I will guard my ways, less I sin with my tongue".*

As you begin to guard your ways with the word of God, your lips will be controlled and you will sin less with your tongue.

In other words the word of God will assimilate in your mind and it will protect your mouth from prophesising negative things. Rather you will start speaking positive things into your life.

For example if you are looking for a child, you will lay your hands on your stomach first thing in the morning when you wake up and last thing every night before you go to bed.

You will say to your womb "my womb I command you in the mighty name of the Lord Jesus Christ conceive a healthy bouncing baby boy or girl".

Which ever sex you want, proclaim it. Command it and order it to come to you. Demand for it and ask God for it.

As you are asking for it believe with all your heart that you will receive it and so shall it be done unto you in Jesus name. Amen.

The bible says ask and it shall be given unto you, therefore you will receive all you open your mouth to ask for.

Condemn poverty but believe in becoming a millionaire therefore get ready to do all you need to do to become what you believe.

Beloved, if your need is money so that you can come out of poverty, which the bible says is a curse.

Place your right hand on your head and now begin to prophesy such as I (put your name here) command that from this moment henceforth I will no longer experience poverty in my life.

Instead I will begin to experience riches, since You O Lord condemned poverty as a curse, I also condemn it. Because I condemned it, it will run away from me and it will not have a place in my life in Jesus name.

Now start praying:

- ☐ I bind poverty in my life and in the lives of my generation, up to the forth and fifth generation in Jesus name. Amen.

- ☐ Now open both your hands towards heaven and speak out loud saying my hands, whatever I lay you on from now henceforth will prosper.

- ☐ I will lay you on my businesses and it will make profit in the range of millions.

- ☐ I will lay you on the sick and they will get their healing.

- ☐ I will lay you on the insane and they will get their minds back.

- ☐ I will lay you on marriages that are about to be divorced and there will be reconciliation in Jesus name Amen.

Hint: - Your becoming a millionaire is possible but you need to keep focused on your written goals and plan.

Since you have decided to be righteous, your mouth will bring forth wisdom and your tongue will not be cut out.

Scripture three to support principle #5:

Proverb 10:31 *"the mouth of the righteous brings forth wisdom, but the perverse tongue will be cut out"*.

You are destined to prosper.

Beloved, because you have determined to be righteous, the bible says your mouth will bring forth wisdom.

Wisdom is when you begin to put experience and knowledge together with the power of applying them into your life situation and it begins to yield some positive results.

As your mouth is speaking wisdom, only positive things will come out of your mouth such as "I am destined to set up many businesses".

- ☐ "I am ordained to set up electronics manufacturing companies which will produce different types of electronic products".
- ☐ "I am called to start my own designer's company and begin to produce designer wears".
- ☐ "I am a manufacturer of designer's shoes and bags".
- ☐ "I have the ability to start my financial houses".
- ☐ "I am an investor in real estate".

As you begin to confess these strong affirmations, you will start experiencing directions to these purposes then you will start running these businesses.

Money will begin to rush to you and you will become a millionaire and in no time become a multi-millionaire.

Hint: - Pray wholeheartedly for good business opportunities that can make you millions of dollars in a short period of time.

Remember to use your tongue to your own advantage, confess money regularly and become a millionaire:

Scripture four to support principle #5:

Proverbs 15:4 *"A wholesome tongue is a tree of life, but perverseness in it breaks the spirit"*.

My brothers and sisters in Christ, I believe that you have wholesome tongues which are trees of life and capable of producing something good and I reckon that as you begin to speak to every dead situation in your life they will begin to come alive.

I say bad situations will become good situations for your sake. Stagnant businesses will become productive businesses for you. Those businesses that refused to make you money in the past will begin to produce thousands of dollars in profit in Jesus Name.

That womb that has refused to bear children will come alive and begin to produce children for you. A child that had gone wayward will suddenly become obedient in Jesus Name. A spouse that requested for a divorce and did not want to know you will start looking for a reunion. This is your portion in Jesus name.

That mind that has been tampered with by the enemy, which was not thinking right before will now begin to think in the fourth dimension. You will begin to dream big dreams. And that same mind will begin to think through how to start big businesses, write them down as goals and will begin to act on the goals until they are achieved in Jesus name.

This will then pave a way for you to become a millionaire. The moment your ideas are transformed into products and are out there in the world market that is it. You have made it, and money will start coming into your hands

Hint: - You need other millionaire's experiences. Find a good millionaire who is willing to help you, make him or her your mentor.

You must understand the importance of magnifying God with your tongue, so that He will be with you all the way through to achieving your goals.

Scripture five in support of principle five:

Acts 10:46 *"for they heard them speak in tongues and magnify God"*.

Start thinking and acting big. No more limitations. You are on your way to becoming a millionaire.

In other words as you begin to use your tongue to magnify God in every situation that you find yourself, things will start taking a good shape in your life.

If you find yourself in a terrible financial situation, begin to use your tongue to magnify the Lord. By doing these, you will see how that terrible situation will turn into a testimony of good happenings for you, all these to the glory of God.

And as you continue to praise the Lord, God will give you that business idea that you will act upon which will succeed, yield good profits for you and it will turn your financial situation around for the best.

My brother and sister in Christ, once you begin to speak in tongues and magnifies God, it means the Holy Spirit of the Living God is dwelling in the inside of you.

And if your thought has always been shallow you will start thinking big and acting big with no more limitations.

No evil will be able to befall you. Do you know that shallow thinking results in limited breakthrough?

You are a child of the Most High God and you are meant to experience the Kingdom wealth on earth.

You are meant to enjoy millions of pounds, even billions of dollars and in fact every type of currency on the face of the earth.

Hint: - Be nice to other millionaires and do not envy them. In other words appreciate and celebrate their successes.

Your tongue is powerful. Be mindful of what you say with your mouth:

Scripture six to support principle #5:

James 3:5 "*Even so, the tongue is a little member of the body but it boasts great things. See how great a forest a little fire can kindle*"!

With your mouth call forth your prosperity and become a milllonaire.

Although the tongue is very small, it is very powerful. God deposited so much power in the tongue for the benefit of man on planet earth. God wants you to use the power in your tongue to create your own heaven on earth.

God wants you to call forth your prosperity, healing, businesses, money, breakthrough, and many more with your mouth.

God wants you to call your spouse forth if you are single. He wants you to call forth your healing if you are sick. God said you should call forth your breakthrough. The power is in your tongue so use it.

My brothers and sisters in Christ, I believe that as you begin to exercise the power in your tongue, and begin to call forth your millions, God will bless you bountifully with ideas that will give you your financial breakthrough.

Then you will begin to enjoy the blessings, the joy and money that come with the fruit of your labour. Your businesses and companies are all the fruit of your labour.

Hint: - It is important to celebrate other millionaires and rejoice with them because what you don't celebrate you cannot have.

Allow your tongue to confess regularly that Jesus Christ is Lord as you pave your ways to become a wealthy person:

Scripture seven to support principle #5:

Philippians 2:10-11, "*That at the name of Jesus every knee must bow, of those in heaven, and of those on earth, and of those under the earth, and that every tongue should confess that Jesus Christ is Lord to the glory of God the Father*".

Those business opportunities that you lost in the past will begin to future up again.

You must learn how to use the power in your tongue to release the power in the name of Jesus Christ, and as both powers join together in the air watch how every knee will bow of things in heaven and of those on earth and even those under the earth will also bow for your sake.

And also watch how every tongue which has previously said no to your request in the past will begin to say yes as they are confessing that Jesus Christ is Lord to the glory of God the Father.

If you are an applicant looking for a job as your conveyance vehicle to your own business, those employers that said no initially will begin to say yes to you. Those business opportunities that you lost will begin to come back to you again in Jesus name.

The womb that refused to bear a child in the past will become productive and bear children in multiples. Those diseases that refused to go in the past will begin to flee from you in Jesus name.

I command that those "born again brothers and sisters that have refused to marry you in the past will begin to propose to you. Those banks that have refused to give you mortgage for your real estate business in the past will write you favorable letters. And in no time your real estate business will start making millions.

Hint: - People are making a lot of money as information entrepreneurs think about it. Make your research and start your own firm in this area.

CHAPTER SIX

Principle #6: You must be generous

The fact remains that a generous soul will be made rich.

Scripture one to support principle #6:

Proverbs 11:24-25, "*The one who scatters, yet increases more; and there in one who withhold more than is right, but it leads to poverty. The generous soul will be made rich, and he who waters will also be watered himself.*"

Scatter to increase more

The fact that there will always be people in need requires you and I to be generous.

The bible says that he who scatter increases more, and he who withhold leads to poverty.

My prayer is that you will go with me in the spirit so that you can understand this scripture, because whoever looks at this scripture with the eyes of the flesh and blood will miss the blessings attached to it.

Looking at it with earthly eyes, one will begin to reason in the flesh and start thinking, how can somebody who scatters increase? It is the truth, "When you scatter you will increase".

When you begin to scatter, in other words when you start releasing and blessing people with what you have, you will be blessed even beyond your imaginations. You will receive Blessings from those places you least expected it from.

Use what you have right now to get what you want. See what I call the Bimbolic formula 4 of God's law.

The Bimbolic formula 4 of God's law states that

4 – 4 = 400 and not 0

Let us look into God's formula which says 4 - 4 = 400. With God's principles if you have 4 things and you release it as a seed into a wet ground, it will come back to you as a harvest.

It comes back a hundred fold which will become 4 x 100 = 400 not 4 – 4 = 0. 4 – 4 = 0 is the formula with the human understanding.

The bible says the generous soul will be made rich and he who waters will be watered.

Beloved, I will encourage you to start being generous from today. This is because I have never seen a generous person who is poor they always have more. The generous mind increases more in all areas of life.

Many are even fasting to get rich. But God has given you an easier key to riches in his word. He says *"Is this not the fast that I have chosen: To loose the bonds of wickedness, To undo the heavy burdens, To let the oppressed go free, And that you break every yoke? Is it not to share your bread with the hungry, And that you bring to your house the poor who are cast out; When you see the naked, that you cover him, And not hide yourself from your own flesh?"*

Brethren, generous people increase more, they prosper more, they make more money and as they give to the motherless children, God multiplies their money more and more and they never lack.

Hint: - Leverage with other millionaire's ideas, listen attentively to their advice and comments and do whatever you need to do.

Being generous on its own is a factor to your prosperity and your prosperity is a signal to your becoming a millionaire.

Scripture two in support of principle #6:

Proverbs 22:9, "*He who has a generous eye will be blessed, for he gives his bread to the poor.*"

Be generous to the needy particularly the motherless and the widows

To be generous to the needy means you have automatically placed yourself in a position where God will bless you. God says when you give to the poor you lend to Him (God), He says to you "**Defend the cause of the weak and fatherless; maintain the rights of the poor and oppressed**". "*Rescue the weak and needy; deliver them from the hand of the wicked*" Psalm 82:3-4.

My brethren in Christ, I am not joking at all. Think deeply about what our father in heaven requires that we should do.

Take a deep breath and think deep down into the concept. Do you think that you can fail when you do what God asked you to do? I don't think so, rather, I think you will be mightily blessed and you will become very rich. Act on every single word I have written in this book and you will be wealthy.

Please do not go past a sick or needy person without blessing them.

Brethren, do not go past the motherless or naked child without clothing them. I say do not go past those who need houses without sheltering them. For the bible says, "*Do not go over your vineyard a second time or pick up the grapes that have fallen. Leave them for the* poor *and the alien. I am the Lord your God*"- Leviticus 19:10

I know you might be saying in your mind, "what is prophetess talking about here? Am I the government? Or when did it become my duty to shelter the homeless?

Please do not let the devil steal from you. If you decide to see it that way you will miss the blessing that comes with the act. Beloved, generosity is the quickest vehicle to richness. It is a fast train to becoming a millionaire.

God said I should tell you that when you are generous to the needy and those who are not able to pay you back, it is like you are watering their souls. God said He "*will open to you His good treasure, the heavens, to give the rain to your land in its season, and to bless all the work of your hands. You shall lend to many nations, but you shall not borrow*"-Deuteronomy 28:12.

God Himself will in turn water your own soul in every aspect of your life. Your businesses will begin to prosper beyond your expectation and you will begin to make money in abundance.

You will become a millionaire before you realise it, and so shall it be with you in Jesus name.

Your case will not be difficult for God to handle in Jesus name. Amen.

I prophesy that your battles will not be difficult for the Lord to fight in the name of Jesus, I expect you to shout a good. Amen right now.

Hint: - Make friends with millionaires. Ask them for the opportunity to take them out for a meal or drink. It doesn't cost that much to host one person in a nice restaurant in the west end. I am sure you can afford it, therefore go for it and it will amaze you what you will gain from the act.

Be generous and not foolish or selfish as you are climbing your ladder to becoming a millionaire:

Scripture three in support of principle #6:

Isaiah 32: 5, "*the foolish person will no longer be called generous, nor the miser said to be bountiful.*

Favour of God from every angle of life is a reward from God to the generous.

You are not foolish, you are wise and generous. And for this reason The Lord of Hosts Himself will favour you from every angle of life. He will favour your finances, your children, and all that you set your heart and hand to do.

God will favour and reward you for all your efforts to become a successful person. You will not only hear about successful people or only see others succeed but you yourself will actually taste success.

As a prophetess of the Lord, I pray that you will succeed in **everything** you do in Jesus name. I believe you have what it takes to succeed. I also believe in you and I know you can orchestrate your plans to become a millionaire. Beloved, I believe you have the quality of what I call the 3Bs.

What are the 3Bs?

The first B is boldness: People who are bold have confidence and the courage to start making some good money. They are adventurous and impudent. They always stand out distinctly with no fear. They are always willing to take challenges.

The second B is Brainy: these people are intelligent human beings. They have the ability to organize complex and difficult plans and ideas. They posses the intellectual power and are quick to find solution to problems. These people will genuinely help other people solve their problems. They are fantastic people. Quite open, genuine and kind.

The third B is beatific: These people show great happiness as they help other people achieve their goals and plans. They are known for helping people bring their dreams into reality because they believe in blessing people. They are delighted in blessing people and making other people happy.

Hint: - Make a habit of reading autobiographies of other successful millionaires. This will expose you to so many money making secrets.

Do not hoard your wealth.

Beloved, do not be a miser, in other words do not hoard your wealth because misers are not called bountiful instead they will eventually experience lack.

Apply the principles of generosity to your life and you will never lack again. Instead you will continue to increase and multiply. Your millions will generate to multi-millions and further generate into billions.

Hint: - God loves those millionaires who are cheerful givers. Give joyfully and happily and you will be blessed mightily.

Your wealth and money which you have made in millions will endure because of your generosity.

Scripture four in support of principle #6:

Isaiah 32:8 *"but a generous man devises generous things, and by generosity he shall stand"*.

You cannot go wrong when you are generous

The bible says the generosity of a generous man speaks for him like mercy and it makes him stand. You need to be generous. Trust me you can never go wrong when you are generous.

When you are generous God himself will be generous to you. He will open so many doors for you which no man can shut. God will pour His oil on your money and it will begin to overflow.

Hint: - You need a system that will make you rich. There are so many money making devices out there, think about it, choose some of them and start making money with them.

Make up your mind about giving to the poor people from today onwards and you will never know the spirit of lack again.

Scripture five in support of principle #6:

Proverbs 28:27, "*He who gives to the poor will not lack, but he who hides his eyes will have many curses*".

In other words as you begin to give to the poor and you are generous to them, the word of God promises that you will not lack anything, rather you will continue to increase and multiply.

What does it mean for human beings not to lack?

For someone not to lack, means for the person to have more than enough from all aspects of life. It means to have so many businesses including so many real estate businesses generating money 365 days a year none stopping.

It means to be able to solve so many problems and to have money overflowing to you. It also means to be blessed in abundance to the extent of having so many blessings and becoming a blessing yourself. It means for you to be in the position of distributing money and blessing other people with your wealth.

Do you know that being able to bless other people is a blessing on its own? Please never miss an opportunity to bless someone who needs to be blessed because that same opportunity might never come your way again.

Hint: - Once you are able to manage your money you will be able to transform your life tremendously and become a millionaire.

Even the sinner will be forgiven when he begins to look after the needy. His prayers to become a millionaire shall be heard by the almighty God who calls himself the father of the poor.

Scripture six in support of principle #6:

Ephesians 4:28: *"Let him who stole, steal no longer but rather let him labour, working with his hands what is good that he may have something to give him who has need".*

God will fight your battle on your behalf

Please be generous to the needy, for by doing so, God will never forget you and will surely bless you even more.

He will make your enemies His enemy. He will fight your battles for you. He will not leave you nor forsake you. God will answer you when you pray to Him.

He will answer you twice when you call Him once. He will allow miracles to happen in your life. God will wipe away your tears and will give you reasons to laugh.

He will also give you reasons to rejoice and make a loud shout. God will give you a reason to praise him. He will also be merciful to you and to your generations.

Start praying for yourself: "I decree that God will answer all your prayers in Jesus name".

Some prayer points for you:

- ☐ I pray that I will progress daily on my plan to become a millionaire in Jesus name.

- ☐ I pray that I will not get stuck on one level of progress in Jesus name.

- ☐ God will allow me to possess all the good things I pursue in Jesus name.

☐ I will have a reason to praise the Lord in Jesus name.

☐ I shall excel above all my problems in Jesus name.

Be generous to those in need and see what God will do for you.

Scripture seven in support of principle #6:

Psalm 85:12 "*Yes the Lord will give what is good; and our land will yield its increase*".

The generous person shall eat the good of the land

The bible says the Lord will give what is good to the person who is generous. The generous person shall eat the best of the land.

God says the land of the generous person will yield its increase.

My beloved and child of God, once you start being generous, your businesses which are your lands in bible terms will begin to yield increase. It shall yield thousands upon thousands and millions upon millions in Jesus name.

Your womb, which is a land in biblical terms, will begin to yield increase. In other words you will begin to conceive and start bearing children in multiple.

As a prophetess, "I prophesy that your first pregnancy will be "two boys". The second pregnancy will be "two girls". The third pregnancy shall be "a boy and a girl" in Jesus name. Amen.

Hint: Be aware of where you are now in the area of your finance, but have a clear picture of where you desire to go and start working towards your plan.

CHAPTER SEVEN

Principle #7: you must be willing to pay your tithe.

What is tithe?

Tithe is 10% of all the income you made monthly which you must give back to God in the form of tithe by taking it to God's house or by giving it to charity organizations.

The moment you begin to pay your tithe the Lord promises to open the windows of heaven and pour out great blessing upon you. These type of blessings flow like a river and I'm sure you don't want to miss out on such blessings.

Scripture one in support of principle #7:

Malachi 3:10-11, "*Bring all the tithes into the storehouse, that there may be food in my house, and try Me now in this says the Lord of host, if I will not open for you the windows of heaven and pour out for you such blessings that there will not be room enough to receive it. And I will rebuke the devourer for your sakes, so that he will not destroy the fruit of your ground, nor shall the vine fail to bear fruit for you in the field, says the Lord of hosts.*

Do you know that you can rob God? Robbing God will never make you a millionaire because God cannot bless your rebellion or disobedience.

Beloved, do you know that if you don't pay your tithes you are stealing from and robbing God.

The word of God says in Malachi 8 –9, "*will a man rob God? Yet you have robbed Me! But you say in what way have we robbed you? In tithes and offerings: You are cursed with a curse, for you have robbed Me, even the whole nation*".

Do you know that God actually cursed those who do not pay their tithes?

My beloved, millionaire to be, please pay your tithes and let God open the windows of heaven for you. Allow Him to pour out unto you such blessings that you will not have enough room to receive it all.

Once God open the windows of heaven on your behalf you will not struggle much before you will find your purpose and calling.

You will not struggle before you find ideas that will transform your financial situations totally. You will also not need to struggle before you will find ideas that you can put together as a real product which you will sell and yield millions of pounds in profit.

God says try me now and see. Therefore try God today and you will see that He is sweet. He is marvellous. Try these promises of honey to you by God and you will taste and know how sweet God is. For the bible says "taste and see that the Lord is GOOD". Experience the miracles yourself. You have heard enough about other people's testimonies. It is your turn to experience the goodness of God from today and start giving your own testimony.

Please do not rob God, because believe me you don't want any curse from God. It is a serious matter if one is going through a curse from God, just look at the life of Cain and Lucifer himself. Therefore, pay your tithes and be free from every curse. You are already blessed in Jesus name. Amen.

You will not be cursed by God once you pay your tithe.

My millionaires to be, I really believe in you. I believe you will take your tithes to the storehouse and will not rob God in anyway. As you do this you will not be cursed but rather you will be blessed and you will enjoy a smooth road to becoming a millionaire.

God will rebuke the devourer for your sake and you will enjoy a smooth route to becoming a millionaire.

God also said, in the same scripture, that once you begin to pay your tithe and offerings He will rebuke the devourer for your sakes so that he will not destroy the fruit of your ground.

A devourer is something that eats up ones money or blessings hungrily or greedily. It destroys blessings and prosperity.

A devourer absorbs people's attention, and distracts them in such a way that they never focus on anything good that could give them financial freedom.

A devourer makes sure that its victims never finish a project or product. An unfinished product is an uncompleted project which can never get to the market therefore it never turns into money.

Beloved, you will focus on every goal that you have set which will deliver your financial breakthrough. No devourer will be able to eat your effort. The devourer will not be able to eat up your thinking in Jesus name.

I decree that no devourer will be able to eat your ideas. You will get to your destination. You will become a millionaire by the grace of God. Amen.

Hint: - Remember money is the wage of solving problems.

It is a command from God to you and I that we must pay our tithes.

Scripture two in support of principle #7:

Deuteronomy 14:22, *"You shall truly tithe all the increase of your grain that the field produces year by year".*

Give unto God what belong to Him and unto human being what belongs to them and have a peaceful ride to your destination of becoming a millionaire.

In other words, 10% of all the increase on our production belongs to God. We must take it to the storehouse. God's storehouse may mean the church. It may be to look after the needy or to provide education for motherless children. God's storehouse may mean to feed the people who are hungry or to shelter people who are homeless and many more.

My brethren, 10% of any money that comes into your hands is not yours, biblically it belongs to God. Let's learn the principles of giving to God what belongs to Him and unto Cesar what belongs to Cesar. And as you begin to do these you shall surely see the mighty hand of God on everything you lay your hand on.

Hint: - Why not think big and own a distribution centre that will entail other distribution firms? Go for it. You can do it. Do not let fear keep you back and rob you of your success.

God wants to make you a millionaire but you must obey what He says about tithing

Scripture three in support of principle #7:

Deuteronomy 26:12-13, "*When you have finished laying aside all the tithe of your increase in the third year the year of tithing and have given it to the Levites, the strangers, the fatherless, and the widow, so that they may eat within your gates and be filled, then you shall say before the Lord your God, I have removed the holy tithe from my house, and also have given them to the Levites, the stranger, the fatherless, and the widow according to all your commandments which you have commanded me. I have not transgressed your commandments nor have I forgotten them*".

Paying your tithe is a form of being obedient to God's commandment. Once God says it you must obey. That means you are obedient and God is pleased when we obey Him. It makes Him declare us as His own obedient children. He also promises to bless us abundantly.

Hence, you will be blessed in everything you do or lay your hands on to do.

Your businesses will yield 100% profit.

God says you can actually use your tithe to help and bless the strangers, the fatherless, and the widow, and only after that can you come before the Lord and tell Him that you have obeyed His commandment.

God will then multiply the remaining 90% in your hand by a 100%, and that means when you start a business with 90%, it will yield a 100% profit, and as you repeat the cycle God will continue to multiply it for you and in no time you will become a multi millionaire.

My prayer is that you will catch the understanding of this principle in your spirit and put yourself in the position where God will continue to multiply and prosper you so that you will not labour in vain, in Jesus name Amen.

Hint: - Do not slave for money rather let your money slave for you. Be wise make your money work for you, even while you are on the beach, enjoying yourself with your loved ones. Make your money work for you.

There is the need to pay your tithe in obedience to God's commandment:

Scripture four in support of principle #7:

2 Chronicles 31:5 *"As soon as the commandment was circulated, the children of Israel brought in abundance the first fruit of grain and wine, oil and honey and of all the product of the field; and they brought in abundantly the tithe of everything"*.

Ladies and Gentlemen, from the above scripture, we are able to see clearly how the people of Israel obeyed the commandment of God. I am sure we all understood how they enjoyed the fruits of being obedient.

Prayer section

Beloved, my prayer for you is that you will begin to listen to your inner mind so you can hear what God wants you to do in order for you to cross over to your promise land.

A land flowing with milk and honey in abundance. A land where there will be no more lack in your life. A promised land is where there is abundance of everything in life. It is a land where money will no longer be a problem to you, but instead how to spend it.

It is a land where you will have millions of pounds awaiting to be sent in your bank account.

It is a land where you have so much money in your account awaiting to be used to promote and sponsor the gospel of Jesus Christ.

A promised land is a land where you will be able to say Yea! Here I am with a cheque of £100,000 pounds in contributions to building this hospital were the sick will be healed. It is a land where sheltering the homeless will no longer be a problem for you.

Brothers and sisters, this land is closer to you than you can ever imagine. I am glad to announce to you that God is taking you places, He is about to fulfil His financial promises in your lives.

God is about to move you from a place of lack into a place of plenty. I pray that after getting in contact with this book your life will never be the same again, and my joy is for you to become a multi millionaire.

Hint: - Belief that money is good and it is alright for you to have some for yourself. Believe that there is enough money in the universe to go around everybody.

In order for you to truly enjoy your blessings of becoming a millionaire, it is mandatory that you pay your tithes:

Scripture five in support of principle #7:

2 Chronicles 31:6 *"And the children of Israel and Judah, who dwell in the cities of Judah, brought the tithes of oxen and sheep; also the tithes of the holy things which were consecrated to the Lord their God they laid in heaps"*.

Tithing is the spiritual access to your financial breakthrough and becoming a millionaire

Tithing is a commandment from God to every human being; in fact it is a commandment right from the creation of man. It is a symbol of automatic blessings from God to human.

Although we lost that automatic blessing when the first Adam fell at the Garden of Eden, but we regained it when the second Adam (the Lord Jesus Christ) came. Beloved, may I bring it to your notice that your tithes pave the way for you to be closer to your financial breakthrough.

In other words, your tithes will make your journey to becoming a millionaire closer and faster. You must look at your wealth as a sort of spiritual stewardship. You should believe that God gave you the money, and it wasn't yours, you are just a caretaker over it. Always feel a duty to manage it for the betterment of others.

Also, your tithe gives you automatic blessings and this is clearly shown evidence in the next scripture we are going to look into.

Hint: - You need the power to stay with your ideas, set up a plan and play it that way until you achieve your goal. Start playing it your own way. You do not need permission from anybody to start, just start and you will be surprised as others will begin to follow your laws and principles. Remember leaders, start and others will follow.

Scripture six in support of principle #7:

2 Chronicles 31:8, "*And when Hezekiah and the leaders came and saw the heaps (tithes), they blessed the Lord and His people Israel*".

Receive your double blessing now.

Basically, once you pay your tithes both God and human beings will bless you. Your tithe provokes an instant blessing from God. God will favour you with people who are necessary on your journey to become a millionaire. These people will help you and also bless you. Blessings await you all the way through.

Hint: - Feed your mind with positive beliefs about money on your way to becoming a perfect millionaire. Negative belief leads to fear, and fear is human being's greatest obstacle to living a fulfilled, successful and purposeful life.

God attached a big importance to tithing:

Scripture seven in support of principle #7:

Luke 17:12, *"I fast twice a week; I give my tithes of all that I possess"*.

You will no longer miss your opportunities to become a millionaire. Many of us have missed so many opportunities in the past.

God loves those believers who tithe. He will prosper you beyond your wildest imagination when you pay your tithes.

God is delighted in the prosperity of the believers who are obedient to Him with their tithes.

In other words, God is happy when His people pay their tithes. He allows them to make millions of dollars, in fact billions because He knows that blessing an obedient child is blessing a whole nation of obedient people.

God will work with you and make sure that you become a millionaire by opening your mind into better things that will take you from where you are right now to where you need to be in order to be blessed and become a blessing to other people.

God will make opportunities come your way and at the same time make sure that you do not miss these opportunities. As a prophetess of the Lord Jesus, "I pray that from this moment henceforth you shall not miss your vital opportunities any longer. Every single opportunity which was meant to benefit you which you have missed will come back to you in Jesus name. Amen".

I pray that opportunities of divine open doors will come your way. Business opportunities shall knock on your door. Ideas that will bring you millions of pounds will be your portion.

From this moment on, "I command and decree that you will begin to prosper and will continue to prosper, and also recover all that you have lost in the past in Jesus name. Amen.

Hint: Remember, in order to become a millionaire, you need to think and act like a millionaire, so that you will be able to have your millions. If you are not able to think and act like one, then you might not become one.

CHAPTER EIGHT

Principle #8: you must be willing to fast regularly.

Before you can achieve a supernatural breakthrough, you need to combine your prayers with fasting.

Scripture one in support of principle #8:

Joel 1:14, *"Consecrate a fast, call a sacred assembly; gather the elders, and the inhabitants of the land into the house of the Lord your God and cry out to the Lord"*.

You need to deal with those spiritual strongholds on your finance and become a millionaire.

My brothers and sisters in Christ Jesus, let us learn how to get supernatural solution to all difficult problems. Do you know spiritually that sometimes it is not even our own fault that we are poor? Do you know that it could be a spiritual stronghold?

You cannot fight this type of battle in flesh and blood. You need to go into spiritual warfare. You need to fast and pray. Beloved, you need some serious night vigils.

And as you persevere with fasting and prayer, you will see the strongholds being broken down and only then will you be able to get your financial breakthrough.

Beloved, please do not underestimate the power of fasting. Through fasting you will see your financial giants fall. Your financial mountains will melt away and then you will begin to enjoy your financial freedom as business opportunities will begin to come your way.

Through fasting, prayers and night vigils, ideas to become an entrepreneur will come into your mind. So also will ideas to be in charge of many businesses and how to become a multi dimensional business director with a whole lot of employees working for you.

You will have ideas on how to become an information entrepreneur, selling information over the internet and everywhere. You will be blessed with ideas on how to become a manufacturer, manufacturing different product, and money will then continue to accumulate in your bank account.

Hint: - Have a passion for buying 'buy to let' real estate. It is a fast track to becoming wealthy.

Fasting must only be between you and God

Scripture two in support of principle #8:

Matthew 6:16 – 18 "*Moreover when you fast, do not be like the hypocrites, with sad countenance, for they disfigure their faces that they may appear to men to be fasting. Assuredly, I say to you, they have their reward. But to you, when you fast, anoint your head and wash your face. So that you do not appear to men to be fasting, but to your Father who is in the secret place, and your Father who sees in secret, will reward you openly*".

Fast and break stubborn strongholds on your finance and other difficult problems you are facing.

Although God wants us to use our fasting to break stubborn strongholds and receive our breakthroughs, Jesus warned that when we fast and we let every one know that we are fasting we have already got our rewards. Rather, Jesus taught us that when we fast it should only be between us and God so that He can reward us openly when our businesses begin to show up, and money start flowing to us in millions.

Hints: - Form partnership with trustworthy brothers and sisters and start some giant businesses together.

Fasting is very important, even the Lord Jesus Christ fasted when He was on earth.

Scripture three in support of principle #8:

Matthew 4:2 *"and when He (the Lord Jesus Christ) had fasted forty days and forty nights, afterwards He was hungry"*.

You need a discernment spirit in order to distinguish real and fake solution to your problems

This scripture refers to the Lord Jesus Chris when He was on earth. I am sure this scripture will open your eyes that there are some battles that you can not win except by fasting and praying, Even Jesus Christ had to fast and pray.

However, people of God. There is one important thing you need to understand which is, soon as you finish any serious fasting and your prayer is heard by God the Father, who is the creator of everything. The devil will always try to offer you a fake solution to the problem you fasted to get a solution for, so that you will only come out of the problem partially and not completely.

My brothers and sisters in Christ, you need to have a discernment spirit, in order to be able to distinguish the difference between a fake solution and a real solution from the Most High God. My prayer is that God will grant you this type of spirit so that you will be able to know the differences between a solution from God and one from the devil.

Hint: - Do not procrastinate or hold back from taking steps which are necessary for you to propel in the direction of your success.

When we fast and pray God answers our prayers by giving us a solution to the problem.

Scripture four in support of principle #8

Act 10:30 – 31 *"So Cornelius said "Four days ago I was fasting until this hour, and at the ninth hour I prayed in my house, and behold a man stood before me in bright clothing, and said to me "Cornelius your prayer has been heard and your alms are remembered in the sight of God".*

God will send you an angel to meet you at the point of your financial need when you fast and pray.

My beloved, can you see how powerful fasting can be? Do you know that when you fast and pray at the ninth hour God can actually send an angel to bring a message to you regarding what you are praying and fasting about?

God is so faithful and so merciful, and He is no respecter of anybody. It all depends on whether or not you obey His principles. If a son or a daughter obeys God's principles and the father does not, God will favour the child and not the father who is disobedient.

"I pray that as you begin to fast and acknowledge God in all your problems, God will send an angel to meet you at the point of your need. God will send an angel to meet you at the point of your financial need and you will be able to make that multi – million pounds business deal in Jesus name. Amen.

Hint: - If you give the spirit of fear a chance in your life, it will make your ideas to grow and to succeed become that of uncertainty, doubt and of horror.

When you fast and pray I can assure you that your situation is bound to change for good, this Includes your financial situation which will change from a meaningless situation to a millionaire's situation.

Scripture five in support of principle #8:

Daniel 9:3, "*then I set my face towards the Lord God to make request by prayer and supplications with fasting, sackcloth and ashes*".

Millionaires who will show you how they made their genuine money will come your way

I have come to let you know that when you are faced with a financial road block or a financial mountain and you begin to take your request to God in fasting and prayer, you will not only receive your breakthrough but you will also become very successful.

You will trample down that stubborn giant underneath your feet. You will start operating with a spiritual mind. You will start hearing with your spiritual ears. God will begin to speak to you and show you what you need to invest in that will bring you maximum profit.

This will continue to move you closer and closer to becoming a millionaire. "I pray that you will not fast and pray in vain. You will prosper in all your undertakings. You will not lack any good thing throughout your lifetime. Jehovah Jireh who is our provider will provide all your needs in riches and glory in Jesus name". Amen.

Hint: - You must be self-directed and determined to take actions that will make you a millionaire.

With fasting and prayer, you can command the mountain to move and it will obey you.

Scripture six in support of principle #8:

Matthew 17:20 – 21, "*So Jesus said to them, Because of your unbelief; for assuredly I say to you, if you have faith as a mustard seed, you will say to the mountain, 'move from here to there, and it will move, and nothing shall be impossible for you. "However, this kind does not go out except by prayer and fasting"*.

With the key of fasting and praying in your hands, nothing will be able to stop you from becoming a millionaire.

My friend, this is one powerful key to unlock your breakthrough in every aspect of your life. Do you know that with this key in your hands, nothing, I repeat nothing should be able to stop your financial breakthrough? In actual fact, you must also be able to receive a breakthrough in your health, because that disease in your body must become a thing of the past.

Do you know that when you start taking your request to God in fasting and praying you will begin to operate on another level? This level is above the level of flesh and blood.

Remember what Jesus taught us in the above scriptures. It is a combination of theses three things, faith, prayer and fasting, that brings supernatural breakthrough. He says if you have faith as small as a mustard seed you will command all mountains and road blocks on the way to your breakthrough to move and they will obey you.

Although, He also says, that except with prayer and fasting only can you be able to achieve this type of supernatural breakthrough. Beloved, please remember this key at all times and make sure to use it whenever you are faced with any stubborn mountain, giant, or road block.

"May you never quit because of these ordinary and temporary challenges. Because quitters don't win and winners don't quit, so you cannot afford to quit before you succeed". Remember you are born a winner and you will be successful in every thing you do. You are a child of God, and you will live to declare God's glory in your finance as you become a millionaire. Do not forget that you can only become whatever you allow in your life.

Hint: - Do you know that even people who are already millionaires have fear. The only difference is that the millionaires act in spite of their fears. Meaning they know how to put fear in its place and keep on taking actions.

Fast and pray, and command your prosperity to begin. **In other words command your millions to come to you as God's ears are attentive to your prayers.**

Nehemiah 1:4 - 11, "*so it was, when I heard these words, I sat and wept and mourned for many days. I was fasting and praying before the God of heaven. O Lord I pray. Please let your ear be attentive to the prayer of your servant, and to the prayer of your servants who desire to fear your name. Let your servant prosper this day, I pray, and grant him mercy in the sight of this man, for I was the king's cupbearer*".

The mountains, road block and giants in the way of you **becoming a millionaire will all fall flat and you shall see them no more**

Listen my beloved, most times and in real life situations, these giants, mountains, and blocks that I am talking about in the above paragraph are actually in form of human beings or money.

Let us be realistic here, most times when you desire that your present circumstance is no more right for you and you want to aspire higher, it's either you need money to do what you need to do, or there are some systems put in place to limit you. Or there are actually some people in the position of authority saying a big NO to your request.

However, beloved, whatever the circumstance is, the Lord Jesus Christ sent me to tell you that as you begin to fast and pray, these mountains will all fall flat before you. May the Lord give you the ability of the 4As in order to be faster on your journey of becoming a billionaire.

First A means Aspirer. Aspirers are people who have ambitions or strong desire to succeed in life, they have a passion for starting their own businesses and they will go all out for it until they achieve what they have set out for. They will not quit because they realised that if they quit they can not win.

Second A means Acclivity, the people with acclivity spirit move upwards only in their plan to succeed in live, they will do anything and everything to achieve their well set goals. Regardless of what they meet on their way as they are climbing the upward slope to success. They are determined to face whatever the mountains are and bring them down. They will not stop until they achieve their goals.

The third "A" means **Accelerators**. These set of people are the people that increase their speed of success and wealth. They set their goals and follow it. These people are those that celebrate one success or the other monthly. These people run with their goals and dreams, and they are hungry for success.

In fact people around them will always notice them. They set their goals to become a millionaire and follow it very closely and will not allow anything to stop them until they attain all they have set out to achieve.

The fourth "A" means **Ambitious**. The ambitious are full of ambitions. They have a passion for success and prosperity, they never give up, they are persistent. They are also consistent. There is no failure in their dictionary. They never take no for an answer. These people believed that the sky is the beginning of success in there lives. And one of their characteristics is that they are generous to people, so God always supports them and makes their dreams become a reality.

My beloved, you will not aspire in vain. "I say you will not dream in vain, you will not die but remain alive to achieve all your desire and goals".

Hint:- You must stop waiting for others to give you the permission to do what you need to do in order to become a millionaire. You are enough on your own to sanction yourself to go ahead. Start doing what you need to do now otherwise it will never happen.

CHAPTER NINE

Principle #9: You must be prayerful.

This principle goes hand in hand with the above one (Principle #8):

Prayers, particularly those said from 12 midnight, can prevent you from entering into temptations.

Scripture one in support of principle #9:

Matthew 26:41, "*Watch and pray lest you enter into temptation. The spirit is willing, but the flesh is weak*".

We need to be watchful and prayerful as we are moving gracefully towards becoming a millionaire.

Jesus Christ urged us to watch and pray in order not to fall into temptation. Temptation is an incitement, which means to urge or stir to an action, especially the evil or wrong doings.

It is a course of action we need to be watchful and prayerful of throughout our journey in life.

Temptation comes through human beings.

My beloved, do you know that most temptations come through our fellow human beings? Temptation will definitely come our way, especially as we are climbing our upward slope to becoming a millionaire.

People will bring different dubious businesses your way, but as you watch and pray you will not compromise. People would want to put you in terrible situations but as you watch and pray you will not compromise.

The devil will send people to talk you out of your financial goals but as you watch and pray you will not compromise.

People who have what I called the 4Ds and the 3Ps combined never compromise instead they will hang on and stay in their plans until they prosper and make their millions.

What are the 4Ds and the 3Ps, Prophetess?

The 4Ds are **Dream, Desire, Direction** and **Determination.** The 3Ps are **Prayer, Patience** and **Persistence.** People with these combinations of character hardly give in to temptation, particularly on their millionaire setting goals, regardless of what other people around them are saying. They keep focused and they never deviate.

As a prophetess I come to tell you that Jesus said "He will give you the grace to not compromise".

Hint: - People having a JOB and working for others have allowed their employers to place them on a wage. Their employers have also determined for them what they think they are worth in live.

When we cease to pray for others we have started sinning against the Lord.

Scripture two in support of principle #9:

1 Samuel 12:23 *"Moreover, as for me, far be it from me that I should sin against the Lord in ceasing to pray for you I will teach you the good and the right way".*

God not only demands that we pray for ourselves, but He actually want us to pray for other people as well. Beloved, let us cultivate the habit of praying for others. I mean we should constantly intercede for people.

Do you know that when you pray for people it is double blessings? In other words although you are busy praying for people, Jesus Himself is praying for your double portion in all areas and aspect of your life even on those issues that you do not know that you need to pray on.

My beloved, it is sweet to help people, particularly those that can not help you in return. Once you do that, you automatically place yourself in a position for God Himself to help and bless you.

I pray that "God will never leave you nor forsake you. Rather He will help you all the way through until you become a millionaire. I also pray that you will have the desire to start those multi-million worth businesses. I pray that you will have the strength to start your own ministry".

"You will not give up on yourself until you start organising business conferences where you and other business owners are able to promote your businesses to members of the public in Jesus name".

Hint: - Do you know that millionaires have the code to wealth? Do you also know that you are entitled to find the code and crack it? Use your thinking treasure to unlock all necessary doors to your breakthrough.

Scripture three in support of principle #9:

Through the power of prayers God can make the impossibilities become possible for your sake. As God appears to you in your dream those ideas that do not appeal to other people will turn into a money generating idea in your hands.

2 Chronicles 7:12, *"Then the Lord appeared to Solomon by night, and said to him "I have heard your prayer and have chosen this place for myself as a house of sacrifice".*

Your heart will soon rejoice over your becoming a multi-millionaire:

The above scripture is evidence that God answers prayers. I want you to know that every single prayer you have prayed has being answered. You might not yet have seen the manifestation of the things you have prayed for in the flesh, but it will manifest in due time. This is because God's timing is not the same as your timing.

However I urge you to hold on to that prayer and confession. "I say hold on to those prophecies and in no time their answers will manifest and your heart will rejoice". The Lord told me to tell you that very soon you will celebrate some answered prayers in your house".

God said "you should get ready because He is about to bless you in a way that you have never been seen before". He is about to bless you with money. You will be blessed abundantly and bountifully in all areas of life. God will bless you with so many healthy children".

I say "God is healing all the diseases in your body and those in your families right this moment in Jesus name". Amen. Believe it and you will receive it. Concerning your finance, "you are about to get a phone call that will change your life forever" in Jesus name.

Hint: - Believe that whatever you do to achieve your financial freedom will not fail. Think, dream and act on it. Do not be afraid to start whatever you need to start.

Fear has no power over you except if you give in to the spirit of fear. The spirit of fear is very bad, it spreads like an infection.

God wants to heal your land of poverty and make you a millionaire, so start praying.

Scripture four in support of principle #9:

2 Chronicles 7:14 *"If My people who are called by my name will humble themselves, and pray and seek My face, and turn from their wicked ways then I will hear from heaven, and will forgive their sin and heal their land"*.

God does not want you to suffer before you become a millionaire.

God did not want you to suffer. Even though He has His principles for everything in a format that if you do this then you will get that, but on several occasion human beings will always go astray.

However God is saying that even for those who have gone astray and have done some wicked things, He is still willing to forgive their sins and heal their land provided they are ready to humble themselves, pray and seek His face.

Since you now know that God is not happy for His people to suffer in any way or form. If you are in any circumstance or condition which you feel that is not right, begin to pray and seek God's face about the situation. You will be amazed as God will show up in that situation or condition because He is a show up God.

Hint: - Fear is only a protective mind. It is meant to protect you and not to destroy you by scaring you away from your millionaire making dreams or ideas.

Whenever you are going through fearful thinking, cultivate the habit of stopping for a moment and asking yourself whether or not the type of fear you are experiencing is the type that is worth going through.

Scripture five in support of principle #9:

Pray without ceasing. God will hear your prayers and bless you with millions of dollars.

Psalm 55:17 *"Evening and morning and at noon I will pray, and cry aloud, and He shall hear my voice"*.

Your businesses will blossom. They will be known all over the world and they will yield millions of dollars.

The above scripture shows us the importance of regular and consistent prayer. The psalmist explained that when he prays both in the evening and in the morning, God will definitely answer his prayers.

We need to understand the need for us to continually take our request of that stubborn financial situation to God in prayers, both in the evening and during morning times until the answer to the prayers manifest. My dear believer, take your request about becoming a millionaire to God. Ask Him to show you the best country to take your business to.

Remember, God is calling you to take your business worldwide, not to limit yourself in one country. God wants your business to blossom. He wants your business to be known all over the world.

God is calling you to dream big, act big and create big businesses. As you do this, your businesses will multiply. Your money also will continue to multiply and in no time you will become a millionaire.

A dignified millionaire is the type you should opt for. You will become a generous millionaire.

You need to opt for a peace minded millionaire and above all a God fearing and God acknowledging wealth creator.

Hint: - Many people like to exploit their desire to become a millionaire but are not ready to give what it takes to become one. Remember you are worth more than a billion dollars, so what are you doing to earn your worth? I therefore urge you to wake up today. Reach forward and do whatever it takes for you to earn your worth.

Do not pay evil with evil. Instead love your enemy and bless them in return for a curse.

Scripture six in support of principle #9:

Matthew 5:44, *"But I say to you love your enemies, bless those who curse you, do good to those who hate you, and pray for those who spitefully use you and persecute you"*.

Pray for your enemy. That action will remove all obstacles to your financial breakthrough and you will become a millionaire.

Jesus instructed us that we should do good to those who hate us and we should also pray for our enemies. When we pray for other people, particularly for our enemies, we are releasing cool fire on their heads and at the same time releasing answers to our own prayers. Therefore all obstacles to our financial breakthrough will move out of the way and we will experience our wealth.

All spiritual blockages to our ears and eyes will be removed and we will be able hear God clearly and audibly and also be able to see financial opportunities with clearer eyes.

And as we begin to see clearly and hear clearer regarding our financial situation our lives and that of our loved ones will never remain the same again because it will begin to yield increases from all aspect of life.

Your pockets will be full of money. Your bank accounts will overflow. And your bank manager will begin to set special time aside in order to meet with you.

Inch of what happens to you as a millionaire.

I believe in my spirit that you will become a special millionaire, and as soon as you become that special millionaire, Kings and Queens will also desire to see you. You will begin to dine on silver tables and eat with diamond spoons. Your story will change and your testimony will be great.

People will like to listen to you more. You will be well respected in the society and among your friends and families. You will be more significant and your suggestion on anything will matter to people that matter.

You will be able to make a difference in your community. You will make a difference in your country. And above all you will make a difference in the world".

Hint: - You need a budget, create a spending plan and stick to it.

How to pray effective prayers as taught by the Lord Jesus Christ:

Luke 11:1-4, "*Now it came to pass, as He was praying in a certain place, when He ceased, that one of His disciples said to Him "Lord, teach us to pray, as John also taught his disciples."* So He said "When you pray say:

"Our Father in heaven, Hallowed be Your name, Your kingdom come, Your will be done on earth as it is in heaven, Give us day by day our daily bread, And forgive us our sins, For we also forgive everyone who is indebted to us, And do not lead us into temptation, but deliver us from the evil one" Amen.

Pray for the kingdom of God to come on earth upon your finance and turn you from broke to a billionaire.

Beloved, this is the model of prayer from Jesus to you. And as you begin to pray for God's kingdom to come in any situation you are surrounded with, your life will never be the same again. Do you know that when God's kingdom comes into any situation, it comes with abundance? God's kingdom comes with power, and it comes suddenly.

I pray that "God's kingdom shall come upon you, your finance, your health, your church and ministry, your children, your spouse and all you set your heart and hand to do in Jesus name". Amen.

When you begin to pray this type of prayers, your life will change. There will be a big turn around, and you shall begin to eat the fruit of your labour. You will no longer experience delays. You will become blessed and the blessed will call you a blessing.

Hint: - "As you put the principles in this book into practice, you will move from poverty to prosperity". Remember, the ability to create wealth lies within you. You are the only one who can stop yourself from becoming a millionaire.

CHAPTER TEN

Principle #10: You must be willing to be diligent.

It is important to be diligent.

Scripture one in support of principle #10:

Proverbs 12:27 *"the lazy man does not roast what he took in hunting, but diligence is man's precious possession"*.

In order to climb the ladder to become a millionaire successfully you need to be diligent.

The book of proverbs emphasises the importance for you to be diligent. My brothers and sisters, we need to be very diligent as we are climbing up the ladder of becoming a millionaire.

To be diligent means to be careful and to be hard working. It means to show care and effort as you are going into a win/win attitude to life, believing that when your brother wins then you also win. And as you are diligent and obedient to

God, He will give you the wisdom to carry on until you are successful.

Hint: - Remember, not every body will understand your dream or see your vision the same way as you do. Many people will even criticise you but in spite of negative comments, you must take your stand and protect your dream.

God created you to be a diligent human beings. It is in you. I believe your hands will make you rich and you will become a millionaire.

Scripture two in support of principle #10:

Proverbs 10:4, "*He who has a slack hand becomes poor, but the hand of the diligent makes rich*".

God is a show up God. Pray and He will show up for you. We need to be diligent and prayerful in all our undertakings and God will show up for us. God will speak to you and give you ideas on how to write that book that you have always wanted to write. He will show you how to start that business that you have being wanting to start.

You will understand how to start that ministry that you wanted to start. Everything will begin to come together for your sake.

That multi-million pound idea will manifest into a product that will bless the whole world and solve so many problems.

God will give you ideas that will make your name known to the whole world. For he said to Abraham, Genesis 12:2, I will make you into a **great** nation and I will bless you. I will make your **name great**, and you will be a blessing. That is what God wants to do for you also. Receive it in faith in Jesus name.

Hint: - Do you know that with good multi-level marketing businesses and high profit yielding investments, you can live a lifestyle without having to work again?

Because you have decided to be diligent, your hands will rule and make millions.

Scripture three in support of principle #10:

Proverbs 12:24, "*the hand of the diligent will rule, but the lazy man will be put to forced labour*".

Give bibles out as gifts to people and watch God bless you back with millions of dollars.

My beloved, you must make sure that your hands are diligent. By so doing you will rule a community, a state, and even a Nation. Once you are blessed with many businesses, multi-million pound profit will be generating into your accounts on a daily or monthly basis whichever one you have chosen.

And with your money you will be able to rule nations by building the biggest hospitals where sick people will be nursed and cared for. You will also be able to build that multi storey 500 flat apartment where the homeless will be sheltered and food provided for the motherless and the hungry.

You will be able to send bibles to many rural villages where they haven't even heard about the Lord Jesus Christ. There are many people out there who need the Lord. God has chosen you to help them. And as you are busy doing that the Lord will be busy multiplying your wealth and you will have financial freedom all through your life.

Hint: - The first step to becoming a millionaire is to know what you want, set up a plan for it and start walking towards it. Otherwise, if you do nothing you will have nothing. However, that is not your portion in Jesus name.

Your soul shall be made rich in Jesus name.

Scripture four in support of principle #10:

Proverbs 13:4, "*the soul of a lazy man desires, and has nothing, but the soul of the diligent shall be made rich*".

God is about to entrust so many businesses and millions of dollars into your hands.

Beloved, the fact that you are diligent means you will be rich. You will prosper. You will be blessed. You will be able to lend money and properties to many nations. You will be above only and never beneath. As you continue to be diligent, God will entrust so much money and businesses into your hands.

Can you imagine how beautiful that experience could be when God begin to say, "that big business opportunity, give it to my son because he is diligent". "That multi-million dollar investment, give it to my daughter because she is diligent, and I know she will know how to handle it". This will be your testimony in Jesus name.

Hint: - Take your life and fortune into your hands. Start running your own businesses and start making that cool money from today.

God wants to grant you a rest.

Scripture five in support of principle #10:

Hebrews 4:9-11, *"there remains therefore a rest for the people of God. For he who has entered His rest has himself also ceased from his work as God did from His"*.

Make your money work for you and not you working for your money.

Let us therefore be diligent to enter that rest lest anyone fall according to the same example of disobedience.

God's rest in the above scripture is different from human being's rest. Do you know what God's rest means? It means that you don't have to be physically at work for money to be flowing into your accounts in millions.

Do you know that you can only get this type of rest when you are diligent? Beloved this type of rest is sweeter than honey. It is the type of rest you enjoy so that instead of working for money, your money is actually working for you.

Through your diligence, you are able to put some strong investments in place, which means whether you are there or not your money is working for you.

When you are on your bed sleeping your businesses are growing and money is flowing into your bank account. Jesus said, "I should tell you that very soon He will grant you this type of rest".

Hint: - Our thinking and the decisions we take in life can either make or break us.

Scripture six in support of principle #10:

Jesus Christ became poor so that you can be rich and become a millionaire.

2 Corinthians 8:8–9, "*I speak not by commandment, but I am testing the sincerity of your love by the diligence of others. For you know the grace of our Lord Jesus Christ, that He was rich, yet for your sake He became poor, that you through His poverty might become rich*".

Brethren, we must love others as ourselves as we have been taught through the word of God. Once the sincerity of your love can be tested by the diligence of others, then you can reach forward and claim your riches. Because Jesus had already became poor for you to become rich.

It is your entitlement to be rich on earth. When you actually put all the principles you have learnt in this book into practice and you become very rich, you do not owe anybody an apology because it is your entitlement to become rich anyway. Just continue to enjoy your riches in Christ Jesus. He will also satisfy you with good health and long life to enjoy the wealth He has given you.

Hint:- Once you believe that having money in millions is not a sin then you have already possessed a strong key to entrepreneurship.

Scripture seven in support of principle #10:

Allow your spirit to make diligent search regularly.

Psalm 77:6, *"I call to remembrance my song in the night; I meditate within my heart, And my spirit make diligent search"*.

It is important for you as a human being to allow your spirit to make diligent search. I know you might say what are all these about the spirit making a diligent search after all I constantly meditate with my heart.

Brethren, meditation with your heart only is not complete on its own unless you combine it with the diligent searching of your spirit.

It is then and then alone that you will begin to see the massive change in your life progress. It is after that you will be able to hear clearly in your spirit what you need to use your money for. What organisation you should get yourselves involved with and what corporations you can buy and make your cool and easy money without any stress.

It is after a diligent searching of your spirit that money will begin to rush into your bank account and in no time you will become a millionaire, you will become a dignified one that God is delighted in.

My beloved, the Lord said I should tell you that "your time has come to become a dignified millionaire and that is why He has placed this book in your hands".

He said "once you begin to follow God's principle as laid out in this book, you will see a very big turn around in your finances. He said if being ill is your problem, you are healed". Receive it in faith in Jesus name.

God said that even "you yourself will not be able to understand the turn around but you will surely know that it is the work of Almighty God". Beloved, God is closer to you than you think. He is the all knowing God. He is the ancient of days.

For this is what God says He will do for you, Genesis 12:2, "*I will make you into a great nation and I will bless you. I will make your name great, and you will be a blessing*" Deuteronomy 1:11, *May the Lord, the God of your fathers, increase you a thousand times and bless you as he has promised!* Do you know that there is a thousand fold blessing? Well, it is in God's word and He desires to give it to you.

Deuteronomy 7:13, "*He will love you and bless you and increase your numbers. He will bless the fruit of your womb, the crops of your land, your grain, new wine and oil the calves of your herds and the lambs of your flocks in the land that he swore to your forefathers to give you.*

Genesis 12:3, *I will bless those who bless you and whoever curses you I will curse; and all peoples on earth will be blessed through you.*

How about that? This will be your story in Jesus name.

Hint: - Make a choice today that you will become a millionaire. Make sure to write it down and read it out aloud to yourself regularly.

CHAPTER ELEVEN

Principle #11: You must be willing to be blessed and ready to receive your total blessing.

Scripture one to support principle #11:

God has promised to bless you and make your name great. In other words until your name becomes "millionaire John, or millionaire Abi, if John or Abi is your original name" God will continue to bless you.

Genesis 12:2, "*I will make you a great nation; I will bless you and make your name great, and you shall be a blessing*".

The provision is all ready for you. God is waiting for you to start enjoying your millions.

This is God's promise to all human beings. God wants to bless His people. He wants to see you blessed and begin to swim in abundance. It is your right. God never change His word. He said it and it is certain. Nothing can change it because He is a God who never changes. For the bible says, in Hebrews 13:8, "*that **Jesus Christ** is **the same** yesterday, today and forever*".

The only thing you need to do in order to be qualified is to obey His word and apply His principles. Once you are obedient to Him through His word, His prophets and prophetesses, and also through His pastors, you will never be the same again. A big transformation will show up in your circumstances.

You will be able to start your own ministry, your own company or whatever business venture you desire. You will make money and you will bless people. Beloved, start operating in God's principles and instantly begin to possess your possessions. It is that easy.

The provisions are already made. God is waiting for you to start enjoying your right. I mean your millions. You have the blank cheques in your hand so start writing how much you want on the cheques.

Take a step of faith today, start your real estate business. I say start main dealership on Mercedes Benz spare parts. Begin to do something from today.

You can become a main distributor of Samsung mobile phones. You can start your own manufacturing company. Do not be afraid. You can do it.

Remember, once you are about to have a major breakthrough, the first thing the devil will send to you is fear. The Lord said I should tell you that "Fear is not your portion. God said today is your day He said He has delivered you from the setback of fear".

He said He is going to work with you. God said "All those business transactions that you have wanted to do but you are afraid to start, go ahead and start them now because He is with you".

Jesus said since your desire is to become a millionaire in a way that dignifies Him, He will take you by the hand and help you until you become what your heart desires.

My beloved, why not start making your money from today? Break the yoke of procrastination. Stop saying "I will do it tomorrow" and tomorrow again you will say "I will do it tomorrow".

Remember with this type of attitude tomorrow will never come and the devil is robbing you of your millions. Bounce back today and take back everything the devil has stolen from you.

You are destined to be financially free. You are too precious to work for people. God has ordained you to be an employer. Do not settle for anything less. You are created to be your own boss. You are born to be a leader.

Hint: - If you truly want to become a millionaire increase your competence. Work on your ability to recognize and seize money making opportunities.

Refrain from known sin in your life and God will bless you.

Scripture two in support of principle #11:

Psalm 1:1, *"blessed is the man who walks not in the counsel of the ungodly, nor stands in the path of the sinners, nor sits in the seat of the scornful"*.

Are you willing to receive your blessing? Get ready because God is about to shower you with a lot of blessings:

Beloved, once you begin to work with God's principles and not walk in the counsel of the ungodly God will bless you. The question now will be whether or not you are willing to receive your blessings and be blessed.

There are many sins in our lives that have followed us for years but God's word says in Hebrews 12:1 that, *"since we are surrounded by such a great cloud of witnesses, let us throw off everything that hinders and the sin that so easily entangles, and let us run with perseverance the race marked out for us"*.

You are in a race. As you pray and wait upon God, He will help you to overcome all such sin.

My prayer is that God will bless you. He will bless you when you are coming in and He will bless you when you are going out. Everything you thought was impossible God will make it possible for you. You will prosper. I say you will prosper.

The Lord of host will shower you with his blessing. You will be called blessed and you will not go short of money in Jesus name.

Hint: - Learn all the skills you need in order to become a millionaire. Practise your skills. Make your millions and help others make theirs also.

You need to have a non deceptive spirit.

Scripture three in support of principle #11:

Psalm 32:2, *"blessed is the man to whom the Lord does not impute iniquity, and in whose spirit there is no deceit"*.

Get ready for an overflow of blessing that will make you a millionaire.

The moment your life is in line with the will of God, God will bless you and will bless your children. Beloved, God will not impute your iniquity. However, remember you need to seek first the kingdom of God and all His righteousness and every other thing shall be added unto you.

Remember that is God's promise, and once he said it, it is settled. God said "you should get ready for an overflow of blessings. He said I should tell you that the property which you had wanted to buy but was impossible is now going to be possible because the time has come for you to buy it".

God said "that womb that the enemy said cannot conceive a baby is now going to come alive and conceive a baby because the time has come. God said your first pregnancy is going to be triplets, two boys and a girl".

The Holy Spirit says, "that those diseases which have refused to heal for a long time will begin to heal, because its time is now over". That disease called hypertension which has been a problem in your life for years will depart from your life instantly". Receive it now in faith in Jesus name.

The Lord said "diabetes will become a thing of the past in your life". God said "heart disease will be healed".

"Arthritis and rheumatism diseases are also going to be healed". This will confirm the promise of God, which says I will give you health to make wealth, I pray that this promise will manifest in your life in Jesus name.

You will have sound health to set those financial goals and you will begin to act on them, and in no time your desire to become an Internet entrepreneur, making millions of dollar sales on the internet will manifest.

You will continue to pay your tithe and God will continue to multiply you in all you set out to do.

You will also remember to care for the needy. You will look after the widow. God will give you a caring heart, and the joy of giving will never depart from you in Jesus name. Amen.

Concentrate wholeheartedly on your determination to become a millionaire.

Scripture four in support of principle #11:

Consider the poor and God will always deliver you from troubles.

Psalm 41:1, "*the bible says blessed is he who consider the poor, The Lord will deliver him in time of trouble*".

Every problem standing in the way of your financial breakthrough, and disturbing you from making your millions as desired, will be taken out of your way in Jesus name.

In other words, the Lord is saying to you that the moment you begin to see the needs of the poor and the oppressed and you start helping them by feeding and clothing them He will deliver you from all your troubles.

Whenever you give people the words of encouragement when they need it you are giving life. Also, remember to give people food and water when they are hungry or thirsty, as you do these, God will never over look your personal needs. The Lord says "He will deliver you in times of trouble".

Psalm 41:1-3, "*blessed is he that consider the poor. The Lord will deliver him in time of trouble. The Lord will preserve him, and keep him alive. And he shall be blessed upon the earth. And thou wilt not deliver him unto the will of his enemies. The*

<u>LORD</u> *will strengthen him upon the* bed *of languishing. Thou wilt make all his bed in his sickness".*

This is a reward from God to people who consider the poor. Any trouble on your way to success and financial breakthrough, God will deliver you from. Your financial breakthrough is now. Beloved, your way is clear. God is showering his blessings upon you right this moment. Reach forward and start doing whatever you need to do and the showers of blessings shall never seize in your life.

Start acting on your goals to make that multi-million business come forth. Call your bank manager today. Tell him about that billion pound idea that you needed money for. Reach forward and start building that business centre.

You do not have to stay in a country where their system is not in favour of your prosperity, or in favour of your business growth. Branch out into other countries that are willing to accommodate you and your business ideas.

My beloved, my brother and sister in Christ, I say "break free and become an international business tycoon". With Christ on your side you can do it.

- Expand your businesses internationally.
- Expand to the United State of America.
- Take your businesses to Australia.
- Take them to Japan or China.
- Why not take those businesses to Nigeria.
- What about Ghana?
- Have you forgotten that you can also prosper in Rome?

Beloved, this is your time. You need to start now. Do not waste any more time. God is ready to start blessing you through your businesses from now. Today is the day, it is the right day to start, not tomorrow.

God said that He is waiting for you to start acting so that He can start blessing you. My prayer is that you will not miss your blessings in Jesus name. Amen.

Hint: - Disobedience to God is the root of perpetual poverty and this can delay your journey to becoming a millionaire.

You will be preserved and God will keep you alive when you walk in obedience.

Scripture five in support of principle # 11:

Psalm 41:2, "*The Lord will preserve him and keep him alive, and he will be blessed on the earth; He will not deliver him to the will of his enemy*".

Reach out by faith and start that business.

Beloved this is the continuation of the Lord's promise to any one that considers the poor. The moment you start looking after the needy God will make you the apple of His eye. He will keep you alive. He also promised to deliver you from all your enemies. Isn't that great to know that God is watchful over you and your family, and He is willing to protect you from your enemies?

God cherishes people who protect the motherless and care for the needy. The bible says the Lord loves them. Considers them and answers their prayers. My beloved, "I pray that your actions will bring you closer to God not further away from Him in Jesus name".

My beloved in Christ, what are you doing about that business proposal? Why don't you go for it? Once you are able to dream about it, it is yours. Your name is written on it. Therefore reach out in faith and start the business. God will see you through.

There is nothing wrong if you control multiple streams of income. That is how it should be. That is how God wants it to be. Jesus wants you to walk in abundance, dance in abundance and have peace abundantly. You have prayed too long for this money, it is manifesting right now in Jesus name.

However, you need to incorporate the elements of peace in your life as you are making your millions.

What are the elements of peace?

The elements of peace are, quietness, tranquillity, mental calmness, prevention or refraining from strife, no agitation, keep yourself calm at all times.

Ideas on the types of businesses you could do.

God is calling you to start that watch manufacturing company.

- ☐ What are you doing about that designer glasses company?
- ☐ Why don't you start that drink manufacturing company?
- ☐ The whole world is waiting for your designer furniture company.

You need to take action and start, so that God can begin to multiply the fruit of your labour. Millions will continue to flow into your purse in Jesus name.

Remember if you continue to do what you have always done and not changed what you need to change, you will continue to see what you have always seen with no changes. But the moment you begin to do thing differently then a higher level of blessing will start coming your way and your pocket will be full of money.

Hint: - take your future in your hands. Do not allow anybody to run your life for you.

Scripture six in support of principle #11:

Psalm 106:3, "*blessed are those who keep justice, and he who does righteousness at all times*".

You will be so blessed and make several millions in such a way that people who never heard about you will smell your millions even from afar.

Once you promote good justice and you are righteous at all times, the Lord's blessing, which surpasses all human understanding, will begin to run after you. Your life will be so blessed that people around you will see it, smell it and feel it even from afar.

And no enemy will be able to stop the flow of the blessings in your life in Jesus name. Beloved, I have good news for you from the Lord. The Lord said I should tell you "that from today henceforth you will start walking in supernatural blessings".

God is about to release a hundredfold blessing on your life and the lives of your children. God said "those prayers which you have being praying for years is about to be answered". He said your joy is at hand, your glory is shinning, and you are about to recover all you have lost in the past".

Remember, one with God is more than a million. Go and start that film producing company that you have always thought about. Start that big supermarket with branches all over the world. Start ordering your goods from Germany and Japan.

I say "start making your cool millions and begin sponsoring the Middle East children's appeal via UNICEF UK or via any other charity organisation of your choice". "Start sending in those donations to help preserve lives and prevent diseases".

Make someone happy today by helping them achieve their dreams and making their dreams come to reality. Give somebody new hope today. Make somebody feel that life is worth living. I say make someone proud of knowing someone who is in Christ Jesus.

Hint: It is important for you to set a time by which you want to become a millionaire.

The Lord reminded us that it is more blessing to give than to receive.

Scripture seven in support of principle #11:

Acts 20:35, the bible says "*I have shown you in every ways that by labouring like this, you must support the weak people*". *And remember the words of the Lord Jesus. He says "it is more blessed to give than to receive"*.

Remember when you support the weak, the blessings of God comes upon you automatically.

My brothers and sisters in Christ Jesus, please remember that when you support the weak a big blessing comes upon you automatically. No wonder the Lord says it is more blessed to give than to receive. When you give to the weak, the poor and the needy, God blesses your finance and He opens the doors of prosperity for you so that you can prosper.

Have you ever experienced such blessings that when you help someone who is in need? Suddenly something which you have being praying about for a long time will just come to pass and you will start wondering and asking yourself what is this that has just happened in my life. God is no respecter of persons. All you need to do is follow His principles and showers of blessing will be released upon your life.

Today is your day. This moment is for you, so get up and start that training company where you will train business owners. Your training companies will allow and enable you to train business managers and directors on what they need to know in order to drive customers to their businesses.

Then you will charge them your worth. I'm sure they will be willing to pay you for your services, because your training is solving their problems. Apply for your TV hosting Licence and start your own channel, where you will teach men, women and children the word of God. It is time for you to start winning souls into the Kingdom of God. Beloved start your own bible school.

My dear sister, start your own ministry where you will pray and counsel people, where you will encourage the broken hearted and reunite marriages which the enemy is fighting and are about to separate, where you will also be able to counsel families which are already separated and reunite them together.

Be very nice on your way to becoming a millionaire. It is important to enjoy your ride to where you are going and keep enjoying yourself while you are there. Remember, no joy is as great as a joy derived from been generous, particularly to those in need. My millionaires and millionaires to be, stay blessed and remain highly favoured in Jesus name.

Hint: - you must try very hard and make sure you become a millionaire within your set time frame.

CHAPTER TWELVE

Principle #12: Be willing to put your trust in God and rely totally on Him.

Scripture one in support of principle #12:

If you want to truly become a millionaire, you need to commit your ways to the Lord.

Psalm 37:5, "*Commit your way to the Lord, trust Him, and He shall bring it to pass*".

"That Gold company that you have being wanting to start is about to spring up".

Do you know that if you commit your ways to the Lord and trust Him, He will bring all your desires to pass? Beloved, commit your desire to start building that factory to God and see it completed and come to past.

Once you put your total trust in the Lord, that gold company will soon spring up. Money will soon start rushing into your bank accounts in millions in Jesus name. I want you to believe that there is nothing impossible for you to achieve. For if God be for you who can be against you? Also remember that one with God is more than a million.

As a prophetess of the Lord Jesus Christ "I pray that as you begin to have complete trust in God your life will never be the same again. God will make a way for you where others are finding it difficult to breakthrough. Whatever business you lay your hands on will prosper".

You will make millions, and once you continue to pay your tithe, God will continue to show up in your life. Your wealth will continue to multiply.

You will build mansions upon mansions. You will give shelter to the motherless and homeless. You will feed the hungry and clothe the naked.

God will answer all your prayers. You will be on top only and never be underneath. Your name will be great. Your businesses will multiply. People in power will give you millions of pounds worth of contract. God will make you successful.

Yes! There is no doubt about it, God will do His own part but you must also do yours. You must try to be an informed millionaire. In other words you must make good research of any business you are going to put your money on.

Before you start any business it is wise to go on the internet and find out some information about the business.

Go to Google search engine, type in whatever topic you are interested in finding out, then press enter and you will be surprised at how much information you will be able to retrieve from a single search.

Hint: - As a millionaire to be, you must use investment growth tools as a ladder to your goal.

Scripture two in support principle #12:

Never lean on your own understanding alone.

Proverbs 3:5 "trust in the Lord with all your heart, and lean not on your own understanding.

Learn what it takes to be an accredited investor:

The bible warns and also stretches the importance of people putting their trust in God. We must never lean on our own understanding at any time. People of God remember God is the all knowing, He is the omnipotent, which means all powerful.

God is also omniscient meaning knowing everything. Why not put your trust in the only God who can never make a mistake, the most powerful one and then leave everything in His care and rest. One thing I know is that He will work in your favour and He will never let you down.

God will always protect your interest. Most people fall flat and failed woefully because they lean on their own understanding. They think they have the solution to all the questions only to find out, most times when it is too late that they are wrong.

Commit all your ways into God's hands and trust in Him totally with no doubt in your mind then you will start seeing great changes. That stubborn disease that refused to heal, commit and trust it unto the omniscient and watch what will happen.

That womb that has refused to bear fruits, commit and cast it onto the Lord. I say "that business opportunity which people in power are refusing you, commit and trust it onto the omnipotent". You then rest your mind and see God perform His miracle in your life.

Give God a chance to do something for you. His speciality is in dealing with impossible situations. Let God work with you as you work for Him.

As God begins to work with you, you will become that accredited investor.

What is accredited investor?

Accredited investor means an expert and a qualified person in stock exchange investment.

Do you know that not everybody is qualified as an accredited investor? In actual fact a research carried out in America shows that only 2.4% of the world population is qualified as an accredited investor. Research has shown that for someone to be qualified as an accredited investor you need an annual income of at less $210,000 as an individual or $320,000 as a couple or $1 million net worth.

That requirement seems a lot but beloved, I see you as an accredited investor. You will be there sooner than you thought. God will make ways for you. You will soon be among the first 10% of the population who control the wealth of the whole world. God is about to burst your bank accounts with billions of dollars. Your name is about to be heard worldwide in Jesus name.

Hint: - You must not focus only on making money, and remember you must not worship money.

You will make your millions definitely, there is no doubt about it but you must be careful not to trust in your riches.

Scripture three in support principle #12:

Mark 10:24, "*And the disciples were astonished at His words. But Jesus answered again and said to them, Children, how hard it is for those who trust in riches to enter the kingdom of God?*".

When you become a millionaire, trust in God and not in your millions:

There is no doubt about you becoming a millionaire once you follow the principles in this book because it is Holy Spirit inspirited. The Holy Spirit troubled me for a long time before I accepted to write this book and bring it into your hands.

When you get to the top of the ladder and you are a millionaire, do not put your trust in your riches rather put your trust in God Almighty who provided you with all the millions in the first place.

And as you put your trust in Him He will continue to direct your steps and you will go from great to greater. Once you are now at the highest level on the wealth ladder, you will watch your money work for you even while you are in the air, travelling to places or when you are out there in the garden with a glass of wine relaxing, your money will be busy working for you.

You must trust in the Lord and promote good always.

Scripture four in support of principle #12:

Psalm 37:3, *"Trusts in the Lord and do good, dwell in the land and feed on His faithfulness"*.

God never fails! So try His alternative therapy:

Once we are able to trust God and do good, then we should dwell in the land and feed on God's faithfulness. God never fails. Watch how all those problems that you have prayed about and now committed into God's hand will be solved, because He never fails. Our mother, father, sisters and brothers may let us down but Jesus never fails.

Coming to God and trusting Him with all your cares is the best alternative therapy you have ever chosen and the best choice you have ever made. Congratulations! All those problems are coming to an end very soon.

Do you know that you can have high quality retail companies where you buy stuff from the manufacturers at whole sales and distributor's prices and resell them at retail prices? This is your day, now is your time, start immediately.

Stop wasting time. You will be glad you get started. Do not listen to that negative thought from your mind saying you can not do it. Stop listening to those negative people around you saying you can't do it. Do not listen to those people asking you who do you think you are, and how do you think you can handle that big project.

You just go and find out what you need to do and start doing it and in no time those same people will come to your house to congratulate you. Your joy will overflow. You will bring good testimonies to the church and you will also bless the church.

Beloved, you are special in the sight of God. God is willing to turn your sorrow into joy. He wants to make you happy. He wants to change your name from sadness to happiness. God is about to change your cry to laughter. Rejoice because blessing is knocking at your door.

Your God is about to move in a great way. He wants to shut the mouth of the enemy forever. That business that looks dead is about to resurrect.

That same business will start booming. Money will start rolling in to your hands in millions.

Listen to me beloved, that child that ran out of the house is about to resurrect because he is on his way back home to you.

That husband that does not want to see you is about to resurrect because he is now telling friends and family to come to you and plead on his behalf because he now realised your worth.

Those people that thought you were nobody now wants you back as their best friends because they can now see your future. All your enemies are about to reconcile with you. You are about to arrive at your destined positions.

Make God your hope.

Scripture five in support of Principle #12:

Psalm 71:5, *"for you are my hope, O Lord God; You are my trust from my youth"*.

God is delighted when you make Him your hope. He wants you to put your trust in Him right from your youth. And once you do that, God will prove Himself worthy to be praised. Remember, He is worthy to be worshipped. The bible says "He is King of kings and the Lord of lords".

Trust God and rely upon him.

Hints: - Have you been thinking about starting your wrist watch company? Today is your day, go to Switzerland and start making your connections. Buy the watches in bulk and at wholesales prices, start selling at retail prices and start making your profits.

Are you thinking about selling designer shoes and bags? Make your trip to Italy. Design your products and start selling them. Your reward is the profits.

Is it lace material you want to sell? Arrange your trips to Holland, go to Swiss where you can make large purchases and start selling at retail prices. Remember to put your warehouse on the high street, because location matters when it come to selling.

Whatever be your dream, that you have being thinking of starting for years, start now. Today is the day you have being waiting for trust in Him right from your youth. And once you do that, God will prove Himself worthy to be praised. Remember, He is worthy to be worshipped. The bible says "He is King of kings and the Lord of lords".

Scripture six in support of principle #12:

Isaiah 50:10 says *"Who among you fears the Lord? Who obeys the voice of His servant? Who walks in darkness and has no light? Let him trust in the name of the Lord and rely upon his God"*.

My beloved, now that you understood the first principle from this book, I believe that you have started to seek first the kingdom of God. I want to let you know that the days of sorrow are over in your life. Walking in darkness I believe is also a thing of the past.

The bible says my people are perishing due to lack of knowledge. I pray that as you continue to read this book, God will give you the knowledge and understanding of himself. He will open your eyes to see Him more clearly. I say "God will open your ears and you will begin to hear from Him more audibly".

My beloved in Christ Jesus, I urge you to trust in the name of the Lord and rely upon Him. Then wait and see the difference this will bring to your life. God is looking for people who are trustworthy and are ready to put their trust in Him. Make yourself available for God now.

God wants to surprise the whole world through your life by performing a big and different miracle through you. This is the type of miracle that the world has never seen before, and will not see it again after yours.

It is a special package for you and your family. It is a package with your name on it. This is especially made and reserved for you. Beloved, do not let this package stay up there in heaven any longer, lean forward and collect it through fasting, prayers and trusting in the Lord.

It has stayed there for too long, you also need to surrender all to God, trust in the Ancient of days and start singing this song in your spirit.

"Unto Jesus I surrender,

Unto Him my redeemer,

I surrender all,

I surrender all,

Unto Jesus greatest saviour,

I surrender all".

Beloved, the days of lack are over in your life. Say it aloud three times with me. 1."The days of lack are over in my life, 2."The days of lack are over in my life", 3."The days of lack are over in my life, in Jesus name", Amen.

Now start dreaming and imagining big and great successes that you want to achieve in your life. Then see yourself, in your dream, actually achieving these great successes. Put it in front of God and trust in him. Then ask the Holy Spirit to work out a plan with you. Start to work your plan by putting days and time to each step you wish to take. Begin to act now and make sure you stick to your plans.

The Lord said I should tell you "that by so doing so, you are unstoppable and nothing will be able to stop you until you achieve your goals. Your millions of dollars are about to manifest in reality".

You are the next person on the queue to cross over to the group of millionaires. Congratulations, but you must believe in yourself and your ability to achieve these goals.

Do not put your trust in friends but in God.

Scripture seven in support of principle #12:

Micah 7:5 "*Do not trust in a friend, do not put your confidence in a companion; Guard the doors of your mouth from her who lies in your bosom*".

You need a supernatural power in order to achieve supernatural success:

In this scripture, the bible warns that we should never put our trust in a friend rather we should trust God. The moment we get our priorities right and stop putting our trust in friends or companion our lives will begin to change instantly.

Things will begin to take on a new dimension. God will begin to lead us and guide us in the right directions, and before we know it, success will begin to manifest in our lives.

Do you know that Friends and companions are only human like you? You need a supernatural power to achieve supernatural success. Therefore cling unto God. Trust Him and watch Him do wonders in both your life and that of your family. God knows your yesterday, today and tomorrow. He is the only one that knows how to fit in all the missing parts. Trust Him and Let Him do it for you.

You are about to know the secret that dignified millionaires have used for years to make clean money and enjoy the work of their hands. Beloved, the music industry needs someone like you who will use their talent to sing songs that will praise God and appreciate the Lord Jesus Christ. Maybe that is your calling. Maybe that is where you are going to make your millions.

What about the film industry? They want people like you who will write, direct and act films that will lift up the name of God I think that is another area where you can make your cool millions.

The Lord will strengthen your hands and will lead you in his wisdom and power. You will never fail in Jesus name.

The enemy is so crafty and most times when you are about to achieve a breakthrough he will try all he can to stop that progress from manifesting, but I come to let you know that except you agree with him or give in to him, he can never succeed in your life.

I therefore urge you to refuse to listen to the devil because he has nothing good to offer. I encourage you to begin to see the positive side of things and continue to take actions.

Begin to act now and make sure you stick to your plans.

The Lord said I should tell you "that by so doing you are unstoppable and nothing will be able to stop you until you achieve your goals. Your millions of dollars are about to manifest in reality".

You are the next person on God's list to become a millionaire. Congratulations, again I advice that you must believe in yourself and your ability to achieve these goals.

APPENDIX

Prayer points:

1. God silence the voices of my enemies forever in Jesus name.

2. God, let my enemies eyes be darkened that they see me no more until I become a millionaire in Jesus name.

3. Let all the bad things my enemies are thinking towards me never manifest. I send everything evil they have sent to me back to sender in Jesus name.

4. Let my life be successful in Jesus name.

5. Father in heaven, break the teeth of the wicked in Jesus name.

6. Father, I pray that you break their back bones so they will never succeed with their evil plans in Jesus name.

7. I release the fire of the Holy Ghost to protect my finances daily in Jesus name.

8. Father I pray to have favour in your sight in Jesus name.

9. I decree increased vision and uncommon ideas on my life in Jesus name.

10. I possess the gates of my enemies from today in Jesus name.

11. I pray for the grace to be obedient to God always in Jesus name.

12. I pray that I will listen to God at all times in my life in Jesus name.

13. I pray for God's guidance every day of My life in Jesus name

14. I command that every fear in my life is conquered with the blood of Jesus in Jesus name.

15. I command that every confusion on the inside of me be ceased now in Jesus name.

16. I wage war against every enemy of progress in my life.

17. Every power of the oppressor burn into ashes in Jesus name.

18. Father in heaven, please restore back to me every single opportunity I have lost in the past.

19. Every buried talent of mine I command you to resurrect in Jesus name.

20. God fight all my battles in Jesus name.

21. Father let every evil assignment to my life bow in Jesus name. Amen.

DAILY CONFESSIONS

Confess the following scripture daily.

- Psalm 27:1-2, "*The Lord is my light and my salvation; whom shall I fear? The Lord is the strength of my life, of whom shall I be afraid? When the wicked, even mine enemies and my foes, came upon me to eat up my flesh, they stumbled and fell*".

- Psalm 139:13, "*for thou hast possessed my reins: thou hast covered me in my mother's womb*".

- Psalm 115:14, "*The Lord shall increase my family and I more and more in Jesus name*".

- 3 John 1:2, *Beloved,* "*I wish above all things that thou may prosper and be in health, even as you soul prospers*".

- Colossians 2:14-16, "*Blotting out the handwriting of ordinances that was against us, which was contrary to us. And took it out of the way, nailing it to his cross. And having spoiled principalities and powers, he made a show of them openly, triumphing over them in it".*

- Jeremiah 1:12, *"Then said the Lord unto me, Thou hast well seen, for I will hasten my word to perform it".*

BLESSING SCRIPTURES

Finally, all of you be of one mind, having compassion for one another; love as brothers, be tender hearted, be courteous: not returning evil for evil or reviling for reviling, but on the contrary blessing, knowing that you were called to this, that you may inherit a blessing. For He who would love life and see good days, let him refrain his tongue from evil, and his lips from speaking deceit. Let him turn away from evil and do good; Let him seek peace and pursue it. For the eyes of the Lord are on the righteous, and His ears are open to their prayers; but the face of the Lord is against those who do evil.

1 Peter 3: 8-12.

I will make you a great nation; I will bless you and make your name great; and you shall be a blessing. I will bless those who bless you, and I will curse him who curses you; and in you all the families of the earth shall be blessed.

Genesis 12: 2-3

Then I will command My blessing on you in the sixth year, and it will bring forth and produce enough for three years.

Leviticus 25:21

Behold I set before you a blessing and a curse; the blessing if you obey the commandments of the Lord your God which I command you today.

Deuteronomy 11: 26-27

Salvation belongs to the Lord. Your blessing is upon your people.

Psalm 3: 8

The blessing of the Lord makes one rich and He adds no sorrow with it.

Proverbs 10:22

I will make them and the places all around My hill a blessing; and I will cause showers to come down in their season; there shall be showers of blessing.

Ezekiel 34:26

For the seed shall be prosperous, the vine shall give its fruit, the ground shall give her increase, and the heavens shall give their dew- I will cause the remnant of this people to possess all these, and it shall come to pass that just as you were a curse among the nations, O house of Judah and house of Israel, so I will save you, and you shall be a blessing. Do not fear, let your hands be strong.

Zechariah 8:12-13

That the blessing of Abraham might come upon the Gentiles in Christ Jesus, that we might receive the promise of the sprit through faith.

Galatians 3:14

Blessed be the God and Father of our Lord Jesus Christ, who has blessed us with every spiritual blessing in the heavenly places in Christ, just as He chose us in Him before the foundation of the world, that we should be holy and without blame before Him in love, having predestined us to adoption as sons by Jesus Christ to Himself, according to the good pleasure of His will.

Ephesians 1: 3-5

And every creature which is in heaven and on the earth and under the earth and such as are in the sea, and all that are in them, I heard saying: Blessing and honour and glory and power be to who sits on the throne, and to the Lamb forever and ever.

Revelation 5: 13

MORE SCRIPTURES ON BLESSING

- Numbers 6:24

- Psalm 34:1

- Psalm 63:4

- Psalm 103:1

- Psalm 115:12

- Luke 6:28

- Romans 12:14

- 1 Corinthians 4:12

- James 3:9

- Genesis 1:22

- Genesis 12:3

- Genesis 27:29

- Genesis 27:33

- Numbers 24:9

- Deuteronomy 28:4

- Psalm 1:1

- Psalm 32:2

- Psalm 33:12

HOW TO COMMAND YOUR HEALING FROM INFIRMITY

GOD WANTS TO HEAL YOU FROM ALL FORMS OF DISEASE AND INFIRMITY.

Infirmity means physical weakness.

Do you suffer from any form of infirmity? If you do, then receive your healing immediately by reading; and personalising the following scripture; and pray to God about it.

Many are the afflictions of the righteous, but the Lord delivers me out of them all, He guards all my bones; not one of them is broken.

Psalm 34:19&20

No evil shall befall me, nor shall any plague come near my dwelling, for He shall give His angels charge over me to keep me in all my ways.

Psalm 91:10&11

Bless the Lord, o my soul; and all that is within me, bless His holy name. Bless the Lord, o my soul, and forget not all his benefits, who forgive all my iniquities, who heals all my diseases; who redeems my life from destruction.

Psalm 103:1-4

And said if you diligently heed the voice of the Lord your God and do what is right in His sight, give ear to His Commandments and keep all His statutes, I will put none of the diseases on you which I have brought on the Egyptians. For I am the Lord who heals.

Exodus 15:26

THE FOLLOWING ARE HEALING SCRIPTURES:

Do you suffer from stomach or abdominal problems?

Use the following scriptures:-

Psalm 30:2&3

O Lord my God, I cried out to You, and You healed me (of my stomach and abdominal diseases). O Lord brought my soul up from the grave; You have kept me alive, that I should not go down to the pit.

Do not be wise in your own eyes; fear the Lord and depart from evil, it will be health to your flesh, and strength to your bones.

Proverb 3:7&8

- Proverbs 4:20-22

Do you suffer from ARTHRITIS?

Use the following scriptures:-

- Isaiah 35:3

- Job 4:3&4

- Psalm 145:14

- Psalm 146:7&8

DO YOU SUFFER FROM ASTHMA?

Use the following Scriptures:-

- Lamentation 3:56

- Joel 2:32

- Act 17:25

- Psalm 91:3

DO YOU SUFFER FROM DIABETES?

Try the following scriptures:-

- Psalm 103:3

- Psalm 107:20

- 1Peters 3:12

- Psalm 138

- Jeremiah 17:14

- Jeremiah 33:6

- 3 John:2

- James 5:16

- Proverbs 12:18

ABOUT THE AUTHOR

About Pastor Abimbola Cole (Idris):

Her calling is in the area of prosperity, healing and caring. She is the writer and author of the best selling books called "How to become a millionaire in a way that is dignifying to God" and "How to spring from nobody to a millionaire" (with all right reserved). She is a motivational speaker, a coach and a teacher of success skills.

Abimbola Cole is the CEO and Founder of "God Transformation clinic" and "The Lord Ambassador organisation". She is the pastor and Prophetess of God's promises international Christian centre.

Pastor Abimbola Cole is a philanthropist with concerns for the welfare of mankind and building houses for the children in need in the developing world.

She is the founder of "successful philanthropist" magazine and "All round success and prosperity now & for ever magazine.

Before her calling Pastor Abimbola is a midwife with a strong background in medicine. She is also a strong voice in the industry of network marketing.

Her passion is to see the body of Christ delivered from the spirit of poverty, receive wealth transformation and stay prosperous.

She also has a passion for releasing the word of God and seeing the sick receive their healing.

Finally, pastor Abimbola is an editor, a speaker, trainer, coach and consultant on prosperity, healing and wealth creation.

PRAYER AND INTERCESSION

We at God's Promises International Christian Centre believed greatly in the power of prayer and intercession.

We believe you are our family and are ready to support you with prayers and intercession until you get your breakthrough.

Send your prayer request to me on my personal e-mail address

abimbola_cole@yahoo.co.uk and I will continue to prayer for you as soon as possible.

Remain Blessed.

From the senior pastor Abimbola Cole Idris

PARTNERS OF COVENANT

Beloved and faithful child of God, You are welcome as covenant partner to this ministry.

The Lord Jesus Christ has promised to send me faithful individuals to partnership with me both financially, emotionally and spiritually in taking His promises on prosperity, healing and caring to the whole world.

Therefore if God has laid it on your heart to support this ministry in any form, please contact us on www.makemillion. co.uk

Or on my personal email address abimbola_cole@yahoo. co.uk or

Tel: 07946309119

Thank you and God bless you mightily.

TESTIMONIES

If the Lord has blessed you in anyway or form after reading this book and followed the principles as laid down in it, we will like you to give your testimony.

Please e-mail on my personal email at abimbola_cole@yahoo.co.uk

GOD'S PROMISES ON WEALTH

This book will give you the motivation, inspiration, scriptures and powerful ideas that you need to break free from the spirit of poverty and become prosperous as God has ordained for you to be.

After you finish reading this book you will discover the following:

- God's plans for your prosperity Principles of wealth creation.
- How to bring your legacy to life
- Money making ideas
- How the millionaires think
- How to become a millionaire yourself.
- It will show you the best and most successful way of making money in an exceptional, intellectual and creative ways.
- It aims to set millions of people free from the spirit of poverty and teach on the principles of financial freedom throughout the world.
- This book will teach you how to make full use of the talent and skills you have been blessed with by God.

- It specifically tells you how you can make your dream come true and help the less fortunate live a better live.
- You will learn the strategies of becoming a millionaire, and discover what you need to known in order to do businesses that will yield multi-million dollars profit.